The Philippian Fragment

Calvin Miller

INTER-VARSITY PRESS
DOWNERS GROVE
ILLINOIS 60515

InterVarsity Press is the book-publishing division of Inter-Varsity Christian Fellowship,
a student movement active on campus at hundreds of universities, colleges
and schools of nursing. For information about local and regional activities, write
IVCF, 233 Langdon St., Madison, WI 53703.

Distributed in Canada through InterVarsity Press, 1875 Leslie St., Unit 10,
Don Mills, Ontario M3B 2M5, Canada.

ISBN 0-87784-805-X

Printed in the United States of America

Library of Congress Cataloging in Publication Data

Miller, Calvin.
    The Philippian fragment.

    1. Pastoral theology–Anecdotes, facetiae,
satire, etc.   I. Title.
BV4015.M54   202'.07   82-15
ISBN 0-87784-805-X   AACR2

16	15	14	13	12	11	10	9	8	7	6	5	4	3	2
95	94	93	92	91	90	89	88	87	86	85	84	83	82

To Dr. Helmut Niedegger
whose research in the Aegean
inspired the discovery
of this manuscript

FOREWORD

This manuscript has traveled an indirect route from its discovery to its publication. I am indebted to so many for these pages:

To the brothers of St. Thaddeus whose vow of silence spoke thunderously of my obligation.

To the members of my own congregation who encouraged me by allowing this material to be published in our newsletter until a wider audience could be gained.

To Helmut Niedegger—above all, to him—the elusive German scholar whose inspiration I have properly credited in the afterword of this book.

Calvin Miller
Omaha, Nebraska

THE
FIRST
LETTER
OF
EUSEBIUS
OF
PHILIPPI
TO HIS
BELOVED
FRIEND,
CLEMENT

1

The assuming of a new pastorate

1. Eusebius, newly appointed bishop of Philippi, to Clement, pastor of Coos. **2.** Peace and joy and the kindness of Christ possess you.

3. I have newly arrived at my parish, and am delighted at the reception I have received. There is no joy quite so effervescent as a new pulpit responsibility. Everyone loves my sermons, and most are generous in telling me so. **4.** I am preaching my gold-scroll series on the Beatitudes of our dear Lord, and the response has been more than adequate.

5. The church and I are like newlyweds. **6.** We love each other with a kind of ecstasy that can only grow in its fervor. At one point in a sermon they all broke into applause. **7.** One dear sister tells me every week that my sermons are getting better and better.

8. Last week I finally met Brother Glandus of the congregation in Dorsinius. It is not a large assembly, and he has been pastor there for several years. **9.** Some are apparently a little weary with his preaching, and I only wish that he could have a little of the rapport I feel with my flock here in Philippi.

10. Pastor Glandus is in jeopardy. His congregation often protests that he is putting them to sleep. His tonus is *mono* and his tempus is *longus.*

11. He is a fine pastor. His deportment is open and his attitude is good. He loves all men and especially those who are of the household of faith. But his preaching is a persecution of the saints.

12. The days are hard on Glandus. I sense in him the frustration of the disinterest he creates merely by standing up. **13.** He went on a short vacation and the church was packed in his absence. Guest speakers are nearly a festival event for his congregation.

14. There is some truth to the adage that interest is the key to love. Certainly the church is more than a forty-minute sermon. The church is the body of Christ. **15.** But boredom is the enemy of fellowship.

16. It has never been a function of the office of the Holy Spirit to make the sermon interesting, only true. Integrity is the authentication of a sermon and not interest.

17. Glandus is telling the truth, but he takes longer than necessary to tell it. **18.** As certain of our laymen have said, "The mind will absorb nothing beyond the fringes of boredom."

19. Glandus must tell the truth more quickly. If he needs a model, let him remember that our Lord's Sermon on the Mount took only about eighteen minutes to preach.

20. He was able to keep a crowd of thousands at rapt attention. Why did our Lord not take longer? Was it that he ran out of material or decided to save His exposition of the Shema for a bigger crowd or a later occasion? No, He simply knew that interest comes garbed in brevity.

21. I have resolved that my current wave of acceptance must continue. I will make the truth as interesting as possible, and I will tell the truth minimally.

22. Here's the great commission of the pulpit:

23. Take the fewest words possible to tell the greatest truth of all: God was in Christ, is yet, and ever shall be.

24. I am sure I am all the more sensitive to the ills of Glandus since my own new ministry is a whirl of great preaching and long compliments.

25. I am sure your preaching brings on the praise it deserves.   **26.** I hope that one day we can be together and share outlines and manuscripts.   **27.** In the meantime let us both pray that Glandus may survive the fire that gathers about his ministry but is absent from his pulpit.

2

Why Eusebius left Bythinia for his new parish in Philippi

1. Clement, how much I love Philippi. **2.** Glory be added to glory that I am once again the center of congregational esteem. **3.** Phoebe of Phrygia brought us a squab-and-honey casserole for dinner on Thursday. Hiram of Hellespont gave us an expensive scroll of the Septuagint. Publius the Paralytic did his part by bringing us seventeen sheets of high-grade Egyptian papyrus for the epistles I must write.

4. There is no church like a new church. So far, in a single month of serving this congregation, I have been given a new toga, a new tunic and a pair of Nubian lizard sandals. **5.** There was a grand reception where everyone brought snacks to the atrium for Koinonia and Kippers. Yes, I am loved here in the city of Philippi.

6. How well I remember my last year in Bythinia! It was not so pleasant, I can assure you. I only served the church as pastor for eighteen months, but it was a stormy year and a half. **7.** There was a brother named Severus who wanted his son, Constantius, to be ordained as a deacon, and the church refused to comply. **8.** Constantius had little about his life that seemed to merit his name. **9.** He not only kept late hours with wineskins, but it was generally agreed upon that his chariot was often parked in front of the *puellae bonorum temporum* or the "Good-Time Girls,' as Romans are wont to say. **10.** He was churlish and roguish and loose with the opposite sex, but this virtue was his: he never missed church. Still, his father, Severus, wanted to see him a deacon.

11. Constantius had an elevated view of the office. He wanted very much to be a deacon. He spoke of it as being "crowned as a deacon" when it is proper to refer to it as being "ordained as a deacon." **12.** There were some other things that seemed muddled in his understanding. He felt that deacons should be given clerical deductions in the markets of Bythinia. He also desired to avoid the Roman military conscription and receive certain compensations like tax credits of one kind or another. **13.** He did not understand servanthood. I asked him if he was prepared to visit the leper colony to minister once he was ordained, but he declined unless the church could pay him mileage on his chariot and per diem expenses. **14.** The idea of the Leprosarium had some appeal to him since it was on the way to the houses of the good-time girls.

15. I had to agree with the action of the church. Constantius was definitely not the sort of man who should be "crowned" or . . . er . . . rather . . . "ordained" as a deacon. **16.** When his father, Severus, discovered my stand, he became very angry. Severus immediately felt the Lord might be calling me to a smaller parish in rural Arabia. Being a wealthy man, Severus' donations paid much of my wage. **17.** His money was a canker in the assembly. Not only did it furnish Constantius with racy new chariots, but it also gave him the deciding vote in every action of the church.

18. Remember how Simon the Apostle reprimanded Simon the Magician who tried to buy the power of the Holy Spirit? "Thy money perish with thee!" he cried. It was, indeed, a powerful phrase, and one I had much admired.

19. Well, Severus came to me and offered me an arrangement. He promised me that if we ordained Constantius, he would see to it that my salary would climb several sheckels in a single *annum*. **20.** He promised me that I would never want for the common necessities. It was clearly an ecclesiastical bribe, so I also cried, "Thy money perish with thee."

21. Things went downhill after that. Severus withheld his tithe. There was usually not enough money to pay my wage. Constantius finally quit church and married one of the good-time girls. **22.** Most of the church withdrew from me fearing to risk the displeasure of Severus.

23. The other deacons refused to go to the leper colony. I took over that ministry. **24.** As my reputation eroded in Bythinia, I grew more fond of the lepers, particularly Lenia. She taught me that need alone causes us to hunger for Christ. "Health and wealth wean us of our need for Christ," said Lenia. "It is only to the poor in spirit that the Spirit comes," she said. "It is not so bad to lose a wealthy member. It may be that very insufficiency which turns you to Christ. **25.** It is amazing how much I have learned of the love of God in a decade of leprosy. The pain of life best buys for us that intimacy with Christ that money is powerless to purchase." **26.** The membership of Bythinia finally asked me to go. **27.** Having no church of my own, I went to serve among the lepers until the church here in Philippi invited me to be their pastor.

28. Ah, Clement, they love me. They care for all my needs. **29.** But yesterday I was confronted by Coriolanus who has been a member of the church here in Philippi for thirty years. He has a daughter he would like to be a deaconess. **30.** He promised me a consistent wage if I would see that his daughter becomes one. I told him that I would see what I could do. **31.** He would like for her to be "crowned" as a deaconess by the Ides of Janus. I reminded him that the word was "ordained."

32. Even in this sea of acceptance I am suddenly afraid. Coriolanus is a big giver, and in some ways reminds me of Severus. Maybe I shouldn't worry. After all, I seem to be so well loved. **33.** I remember the haunting words of Lenia the Leper of Bythinia, "Only in the poverty of our need may we discover the riches of Christ." May I choose such poverty as will make me truly rich.

3

The unkind outcome of the former pastor in Philippi

1. I am pastor! Oh, the exhilaration of the very words *Reverend Eusebius!* One of these Philippians called me Doctor Eusebius the other day. It sounded so good... Dr. Eusebius! **2.** I was jubilant thinking how it would look in Doric letters on the church sign. What joy there is in being pastor!

3. But some of the joy I would otherwise feel is blunted by the remembrance of my predecessor, Quartus. I watched one of the members with a bucket of white paint taking his name off the church sign last week. **4.** "Is it as hard to erase the memory as the name?" I asked our church sign painter.

5. "Oh, no," he said. "Third time I have painted out a pastor's name in this decade."

6. "Did you like Quartus? Was he a good pastor?" I asked.

7. "Yes, but he crossed Coriolanus... I heard his daughter wanted to be a deaconess and

Quartus refused."

8. I said nothing but swallowed hard. The sign painter continued.

9. "Quartus wasn't really his name, you know. His name was Cato, but it gets easier to call your pastor by a number rather than by his name. Tertius came before him."

10. "What was his real name?" I asked.

11. "Can't recall . . . He only lasted seven months."

12. "Thrown to the lions?" I asked, almost preferring that Tertius had been devoured by lions than by Coriolanus.

13. "Nope, that would have been easier! No, we all heard that Coriolanus didn't like a certain sermon Tertius preached against rich Christians who tried to buy pre-eminence. He reminded the rich that while they might buy position in this church, it was not for sale in heaven. He picked an unfortunate text for his sermon."

14. "What?" I asked.

15. "Thy money perish with thee."

16. I swallowed hard. "Maybe I should have gone to Arabia," I thought to myself.

17. "Seven months, huh?" I asked when I had regained my composure. "What happened to the pastor before him?"

18. "Secundus?"

19. "Yes, Secundus."

20. "Well, let's see. That was the split led by

Demetrius because Coriolanus wanted to be the moderator and . . ."

21. "Secundus preferred otherwise."

22. The sign painter looked at me. "How did you know?" he asked. "Do you have the gift of prophecy?"

23. "No," I replied, "but I can sometimes see trends."

24. "Trends?"

25. "Never mind, just tell me about Quartus, my immediate predecessor. How did he escape Coriolanus' struggle to have his daughter elected a deaconess?"

26. "Well, he looked very tired just before the business meeting when he would have been ousted as pastor.   **27.** He was solid on the point—he would not permit Coriolanus' daughter to be 'crowned.' He wanted out! He was tired of the church and Coriolanus' congregational briberies. So he went through a big crowd on the Lupercal singing hymns to the praise of Christ."

28. "That was foolhardy! Was he arrested?"

29. "Immediately, and thrown to the lions the very evening the church met to consider his dismissal. Things being what they were, some considered it a nice way to go to be with our Lord.   **30.** Many of Coriolanus' camp said it was a coward's way out, but Quartus was not much of a fighter, I'm afraid."

31. By this time he had painted out the name

of my predecessor. As he walked away, I asked him where he was going.

32. "To the marketplace to get another ewer of whitewash. You can't afford to get low on white paint in this church. I've got to keep the sign in good shape—all the names current."

33. I was disenchanted as I saw him walk away. "I have been most popular here in my first few weeks. Surely I have nothing to fear," I thought. "The fates of Secundus and Tertius and Quartus will never be mine," I reasoned as the sign painter left. **34.** When he was all but out of sight, he turned back and called out.

"Eusebius, will it be all right if I call you Quintus?"

4

*A new friend with the gift
of healing*

1. Shortly after my arrival in the city I made another new friend, Helen of Hierapolis. She is a dynamic lover of people, and is so bound up in her love for Christ that she walks in an aura of esteem. **2.** I am not usually so taken with traveling healers. **3.** You will remember my disaffection for Hiram the Healer of the Hellespont who claimed instant health for all who would in faith touch his sequined toga. **4.** He lost much of his following in West Asia because he couldn't get relief from a toothache.

5. But Helen is different. She came to Philippi with a conviction that God loves the suffering and she determined to participate with God in this love.   **6.** I met her near the synagogue when she was talking to a group of blind beggars. I was surprised when she didn't even try to heal them, but bought each of them a new cane and reminded them that the curbs on Caesar's Boulevard were especially high. **7.** She reminded them that they should be especially careful because it is so hard to hear a chariot coming down an unpaved road.   **8.** "Someday," she told them as we walked away, "light will be universal, and every eye will behold eternal love."

9. They didn't feel as though she had cheated them.   **10.** She is not much of a show woman, I'm afraid. She just mixes with humanity in order to take divinity as far as it will go.   **11.** I am the richer to know her.

12. Sister Helen opened a great crusade in Philippi on Thursday, and is the sensation of the leper colony.   **13.** She rarely does anything one could call a miracle.   **14.** Last week she laid hands on a little crippled boy and was not able to heal him, but she gave him a new pair of crutches and promised to take him for a walk in the park here in Philippi.

15. Yesterday with my own eyes I saw her pass an amputee selling styluses. She touched his legs and cried, "Grow back! Grow back! . . . In the name of Jesus of Nazareth, grow back!"

16. Well, Clement, I so wanted to see the legs grow back, but they did not. Poor Helen. What's a faith healer to do with an amputee that refuses to grow legs on command?

17. She sat down with the little man, crossed her legs on the cold pavement, and began selling styluses herself.   **18.** Soon she was talking to him, and before very long they were both laughing together. For an hour they laughed together, and by nightfall they were having an uproariously good time.

19. When it was time to go, Helen's legs were so stiff from disuse, they refused to move. **20.** Her legless, stylus-selling friend cried in jest, "Grow strong! . . . Grow strong! . . . Grow strong!" Helen only smiled and staggered upward on her unsteady legs.

21. She looked down at her lowly friend and said, "I offer you healing, you will see. It is only one world away. Someday . . . ," she stopped and smiled, "you will enter a new life and you will hear our Savior say to your legless stumps, 'Grow long! . . . Grow long!' Then you will know that glory which Sister Helen only dreamed for you."

22. He smiled and said, "Do you heal everyone this way?"

23. "It is better to heal with promises than to promise healing."

24. "You are right, Sister Helen. But more than right, you are an evidence that our Father yet heals the spirit of amputees—even when they will not grow legs. And, once the spirit is healed, the legs can be done without."

25. Helen turned and walked on down the street. She was near the amphitheater where she holds her great crusade when she saw a young girl without any arms.

26. "Grow long!... Grow long!... In the glorious name of Jesus Christ, grow long!" she cried.

27. The girl looked puzzled and looked at her shoulders where her arms refused to be. They did not seem to her to be growing.

28. "I was afraid of that," said Helen. "Oh, well, I can miss my meeting one night, I guess. Young lady, how long has it been since anyone combed your hair?" **29.** And she sat down beside her new friend and took out her comb. For the first time in my life I wanted to be a faith healer, Clement.

30. After the crusade was over last night, Helen came to our home for squab and honeycomb. Wouldn't you know it, she brought a couple of hungry lepers.

5

On positive thinking in disastrous times

1. My joy abounds. The congregation works hard to affirm me. Helen the Healer of Hierapolis is my friend in whom I clearly see Christ. At the moment there is little persecution in Philippi. **2.** One week ago as I passed through the agora on a quick shopping trip, a voice interrupted my thoughts. The voice had a bugle-like quality and had gathered a rather impressive crowd of men about it. **3.** I could tell by the wrinkle-free togas, they were all merchants with an eye to the future. **4.** The name of the speaker was being whispered all about me with great respect—Marcus Sparkus, an up-and-coming Christian motivator.

5. Has he ever been to Coos? He has come to Philippi to lead a cogitation rally. **6.** I may enroll to see if I can add to the Holy Spirit a better mental outlook in the living of my life.

7. Marcus Sparkus has written thirty-two scrolls now, with such titles as *The Impossible Possibility*, *This Way to Success*, *The Zeal Deal*, and the ever popular *You Are Numerus Unus*. **8.** In the first session he tells his eager listeners that God is on their side. In the second he lists how God has given all things and people for our use to make us richer, happier Christians. **9.** In seminar three he instructs his audience to pray for our enemies in such a way that we can triumph over guilt, live a devoted life and become wealthy. **10.** I decided to take the course feeling that it might help my already successful ministry. **11.** But just as I was working out my chart for the future and recording my "Life Action Goals," there was a knock at the door. I learned that the authorities had arrested Sparkus and hauled him off to be thrown to the lions.

12. It left the class unsettled. Now we are not sure about how to make our "Life Action Goals" harmonize with the unexpected difficulties of life. **13.** I do wish Sparkus had been able to finish the seminar and perhaps shed a little light on this conflict. **14.** I did find this curious passage in his *Successful Living* scroll, numerus duodecem: **15.** "We are reminded of the little ant who saw a big, strong grasshopper carrying a leaf. The ant was afraid to try to carry such a large load until the wise old grasshopper said, 'Son, you can do it if you think you can.' The little ant realized that it was not his muscles that were defeating him, but his mind. He began to say to himself, 'I think I can... I think I can... I think I can.' Thus thinking he could, he picked up the leaf and trudged off after the grasshopper. Like that ant, Christians are often defeated in their minds, and they never learn to think in terms of possibilities."

16. Who knows what the epilogues shall be to all these things. **17.** We are not permitted to question, I suppose, if optimistic ants ever dislocate their backs on large leaves or check into their physicians with double hernias. **18.** And what of Sparkus and the big cats in the arena? Can he triumph over them with positive thinking? **19.** One thinks, too, of his scroll titled *Banqueting on the Difficulties of Life* and wonders what will be the main course at the arena the night of his ordeal. **20.** Can he get out of this one even if he thinks he can? And what of his great work, *Put a New Man in Your Toga?* It looks as if they will at least put another man in his, if anything is left of it.

21. I understand he has a group of scribes rapidly copying his new book for publication, which will probably be published posthumously, *Thinking It Through for a Lovelier You.*

22. Thursday night is Christian Writers Night at the arena. I think I will go and see how he finishes it all up. **23.** It will be interesting to know whether in the midst of all the tawny, snarling beasts he lifts his hands and says to the ticket-holders as he did at each of the seminars, "You can win if you think you can," or if he merely cries, "Let me out of here!"

24. I have two more chapters to read in his *Walking into Prestige in Your Own Sandals.* But I keep thinking of Jeremiah who said, "It is not in man that walketh to direct his steps."

25. I am torn between the desire to think positively or to confront life as it is. **26.** If I am prone to remember that Christ said faith could move mountains, he also said that in the world you shall have tribulations. **27.** I like moving mountains and seeing miracles occur all around me; it's tribulation that makes me nervous. **28.** I wonder if Marcus will escape the lions. "I think he can . . . I think he can . . . I think he can."

6

On gluttony and indulgence

1. My first year here in Philippi was earlier eclipsed by a wave of persecution. **2.** But for the moment the church is free; and in the freedom to practice faith, worship sometimes seems less important than it might in more desperate times. **3.** In truth we are enjoying the economic prosperity, although I cannot believe that our good Lord who always cast an eye to the poor would agree with all the various forms of indulgence that one sees around our parish.

4. Persecution has now subsided and there is so little stress that I feel the peaceable kingdom may be about to set upon us.

5. What, dear Clement, is a Christian to do when we have so much that we feel so little need of Christ? Who can say?   **6.** Jesus once blessed the poor in spirit. I remember Lenia the Leper of Bythinia. Perhaps Jesus blessed the poor in spirit because in our poverty we acknowledge need and turn toward Him who is the source of plenty.

7. Now we have plenty and see our abundance rising from our own ability to provide for ourselves.   **8.** The things that God gives us do not cause us to love Him.   **9.** Ever more we treasure the gifts and not the giver.

10. We are made neurotic by having too much. Indulgence stands opposite self-denial and incriminates us with our very love of it.

11. Saturnalia is gone and most of the believers here in Philippi have become confessors of the number one sin of the season—gluttony.   **12.** For a fortnight Christians were saying grace over horrendous portions of goodies that filled out the pleats in their togas.   **13.** Now many of them are waddling off as guilty and unreformed chubbies, unrepentant in their indulgence.

14. We sin so often against temperance, and how comical our atonement must look to our God. My dear Clement, what forms our penance takes!

15. Have you ever heard of the Ovum Fast?

If you eat only eggs for a week while you drink the juice of bitterfruits, you may atone for all indulgence. One hefty believer in Antioch lost a couple of kilos by this method.

16. Then there is the Aqua Concept where heavies lose weight by drinking all the water they can stand for a fortnight. Anna Magna drank forty-three firkins a week while she ran three furlongs down the Athenian Way every morning. **17.** Her weight loss was impressive. And now she lectures intemperate believers on the need for lighter witnesses.

18. Time would not permit to tell all the diets that abound after Saturnalia is over. **19.** Must life ever be seasons of gluttony and starvation? Is there no moderate way to health?

20. All of this is bewildering when you consider that indulgence is a sin which most of us Christians observe too frequently. **21.** How long will it be before all of us learn that overfilling our body is a kind of abuse? **22.** Our Father in heaven created our bodies as the temples in which he could live and be a witness to himself.

23. How good was our Lord's example! When he fed the five thousand he multiplied fish and bread and not sweetmeats or honeycakes. **24.** Perhaps it was his way of saying, "Thou shalt not glut, and he that does shall never squeeze through the narrow portals of life."

25. Forgive me, Clement, if I seem obstinate on the subject, but after all, a witness is liable for all areas of his example. **26.** I remember a portly disciple preaching against strong wine in Berea. His message was abrogated by his own unwillingness to practice a form of denial we all must deal with. **27.** A thin winebibber is no less credible than a thick teetotaler.

28. I, too, am overfed, but I cannot bring myself to drink a firkin of water or trot along the Athenian Way.

29. Prosperity and acceptance make us neurotic about such things as these. **30.** Probably self-control, not the spastic attempt of the overindulgent to fast away their ill-begotten intemperance, is the mark of a Christian.

7

Christian symbols and the danger of syncretism

1. There is perhaps one other evil of prosperity for us who believe. It is the emergence of movements which surround the church with alternate channels for serving our dear Christ. **2.** It seems that various speakers have become popular throughout Christianity, and there are many itinerant spokesmen espousing any number of causes.

3. The faith now fractures and splits into all

sorts of special interest groups. **4.** Now there are a host of popular speakers who come through Philippi renting halls for rallies that center on one kind of partisan Christianity or another.

5. I am plagued. In less than a month we have had a score of Christian artists, evangelists and lecturers come through our city.

6. Titus the Consistent has just left the opera hall after delivering his stunning lectures called "Seven Easy Steps to the Deeper Life."

7. Now Christiana Hausfrau is in Philippi. For only seven denarii a Christian receives three full seminars and a box lunch. She is popular throughout the empire. **8.** Her big seminars are entitled "How to Dry-Mop Your Atrium While You Deepen Your Prayer Life" and "How Christ Can Help You Become a Better Mother and Lover." Her supporters say she is strictly Dunamis!

9. Next week the evangelist, Silas Scorchem, will be holding a crusade in the coliseum while the lions rest. **10.** His most famous treatise is entitled: "Severus Maximus—the Anti-Christ." Those who have heard it are sure that the Roman Senate is the Great Harlot of the Apocalypse. **11.** One of the good things about Scorchem is that his ministry is supported entirely by free-will offerings. **12.** They do ask the slaves to try to be sacrificial for the sake of Scorchem's love offering. After all, it does cost something to buy fuel for the flambeaus.

13. Besides the many speakers who hold seminars, there have been lots of musical groups as well. The "Happy Romans" will be holding a concert on the thirteenth, and the "New Plebians" will be in Philippi on the twentieth. Best of all, "Lucas New Life and the Third Chapter of Zephaniah" will be here on the twenty-third.

14. I can at last understand what St. Paul meant when he chastised our brothers in Corinth. So many are made neurotic by the fans and supporters of each of these renowned lecturers and entertainers.

15. "I am of Christiana," say some. Others say, "I am of Silas," while others say, "I am of Lucas New Life." Right now the "Lucas New Life" supporters are trying to organize a group outing to the concert. **16.** They are, of course, able to get a better rate at the coliseum if they travel in large ox carts and sit together as a group. **17.** Lucas has a special rate for those who sign up to go with the church.

18. Clement, why must the church ever be the pool where all the touring authorities seek to draw the net? **19.** The church, called to fish for men, finds herself in the mindless support of a score of special interest groups.

20. One of the brothers was most intolerant because I would not sit in our special section

at the "Lucas New Life Concert." "Why would
you want to pay the higher rate?" he asked.
"Our Lord always wants us to be good stew-
ards. **21.** Ask yourself, 'How can I draw
closer to Lucas New Life at the best savings
possible?' " he challenged me.

22. Who shall deliver our age from this
fever? How are we to seek the church's inde-
pendence and preserve the integrity of its
people?

23. The lions may help! These artists and
lecturers seem to dwindle when the authorities
begin to scour the countryside for victims to
use at the games.

24. The days sometimes grow serious and
force the church to a focus on Christ it cannot
have while her separate heroes flourish.

8

*How a partisan group limits
the work of the local church*

1. Last week Alexander of Alexandria sent
me an epistle asking permission for the use of
our meeting hall on a Tuesday night. Alexander is one of the Born-Again Gladiators. **2.** It
seems a worthy organization, but I am yet sus-
picious of those organizations which serve
Christ and other themes.

3. Clement, I must ask your opinion. Is it in

the best interest of our dear Lord's love that we support all who wear His name?

4. These born-again gladiators are a case in point. One year ago upon the Lupercal, Bruto the Bludgeon gave his heart to our dear Lord and was, as all said, "a convert to Christianity."

5. Bruto stood in the arena and said before all of Rome that never again would he bash any brother except he would give all the glory of his victory to God. **6.** From this beginning he has been crushing opponents for Christ, and is always faithful to say that it is only because of his Lord that he is able to be a winner in the arena.

7. He is truly an excellent athlete. He is to share his testimony before thousands in the Roma Bowl on Ben Hur Causeway. **8.** The problem is that he is charging five denarii per seat for those who will hear how truly selfless he has become since embracing Christianity. **9.** In this sermon it is believed he will tell how he vanquished Nicholas the Nubian by piercing him with his own trident and crying, "Ah, Nicholas, see how unbelief can be hazardous to your health."

10. These born-again gladiators certainly seem to capture the imagination of the young. But is it right, most excellent Clement, that they charge so much for their testimonies? **11.** They say that Bruto has bought a gilded chariot and rides the streets in pomp since his fee to "share the Word" is adequate to all his needs. **12.** He certainly has a powerful testimony, and being such as he is, no one has the courage to suggest that this testimony fee may be out of character with his calling. **13.** At all costs we must be careful not to make him angry lest he forget his state of grace. **14.** I've never been much for gladiatorial combat. But I realize that all Christians must take up the cross and follow our Lord. **15.** Such following requires self-denial. Woe to all who use the cause of Christ to gild their own chariots! **16.** No, Clement, we are not to follow Him for five denarii per seat, nor for the golden chariot our famous repentance may bring.

17. I marvel that Bruto can sing the martyrs' hymns. Yet he does have a lovely voice which, like his trident and net, he uses for Jesus. **18.** Oh, how our heroes cause us to stumble. I passed a line of truants waiting to get into his rally. They all want Bruto to autograph their broadswords. **19.** Who knows but what one of these little tykes will someday have a great testimony worth thousands of denarii.

20. Still, I would rather somehow that we give our Lord such glory as comes from free testimonies and sermons steeped in the cauldron of study. **21.** In case there is not a Christian gladiator in Ephesus, I beg of you, consider my words, "Heroes of faith are those who follow Christ to His passion." **22.** Let us, therefore, remember: the way to Calvary was not strewn with posters telling how our Lord sprinted the Golgotha Marathon for so much a seat.

23. One of the great athletes of Philippi was converted to Christ following Bruto's dynamic testimony. **24.** He had been injured by an atheistic Gaul who is now popular in the empire. **25.** I asked the convalescing gladiator if he would like to share his conversion experience among our congregations. **26.** "Sure," he said, "how much does it pay?" When I reminded him that grace was free, he simply replied that free grace was God's problem and not his. Unlike God, he had a fee.

9

The acting of compassion

1. Clement, I committed an unpardonable sin. I have angered the Constable Coriolanus. **2.** It has marked an unfortunate turn of events for me. My preaching has fallen on hard times. To Coriolanus, at least, it is no longer acceptable. **3.** My struggle with Coriolanus came to an apex this past Lord's Day.

4. Publius the Paralytic was not expected to live through the morning. Publius asked to see

me at the hour of his death, and I felt it was
my obligation to go to him and "to pray him
across," as he phrased it. He had such a high
fever that it seemed he could not live through
the morning.

5. I prayed for him as I have prayed for few
men. God was gracious! Publius was completely healed.   **6.** How shall I say complete?
He is still a paralytic, but his fever is gone.

7. Back at the church there was consternation that the pastor wasn't there. While waiting for me, they sang through thirty-one
hymns before they gratefully pronounced the
benediction and left the services.   **8.** Most of
them had a blessed hoarseness that they referred to as *doxoma,* a condition which results
from singing too many hymns in a row.   **9.**
Naturally I felt badly. My emotions were mixed
having seen Publius the Paralytic gloriously
healed of a fever.

10. Coriolanus asked me to stay after all of
the others had left the church.

11. "In my thirty years as a member of this
church, it is the first time that the blessed, holy
Word of God has not been preached!" he thun-
dered. "What do you have to say for yourself,
Reverend Eusebius?"

12. "Well," I replied, "I felt that the ninety
and nine were safe in the fold. Publius was
about to die."

13. "Reverend Eusebius, do you feel called

to shepherd this flock?"

14. "I do."

15. "Yet you let the sheep come and go without fodder. A good shepherd would love and feed the sheep. But you have sent them away empty."

16. "But Publius was healed."

17. "Can he walk because you missed your obligation to the sheep?"

18. "Well... not that...His legs were not healed. But his fever is gone. He will live, Brother Coriolanus! He will live!"

19. I can assure you, Clement, that while Publius will live, I am not sure that I can survive the new hostility I have engendered by missing church merely to pray for a dying man. **20.** I was foolish to assume that the church would see the glory of my ministry to Publius and excuse the absence of my sermon. **21.** Through pain I have learned that it is still wrong to heal on the sabbath—at least during the eleventh hour.

22. Is a paralytic worth widespread congregational *doxoma?* Is the yet-paralyzed Publius worth the cancellation of my morning sermon? I have betrayed a tradition to furnish forth a single act of compassion. **23.** Oh, the institutional cankers that do fester when traditions are unserved! If I go on missing church merely to perform miracles, I must endure the wrath not only of Coriolanus but the whole congregation.

24. It is time for the evening vigil now, and I have just received word that one of the lepers is at death's door and has called for me to come. Shall I go to tend the dying, or shall I go to church and keep my place? **25.** I had planned to talk tonight about how we must minister to our world before we seek each other's consolations. I am still unforgiven by most for healing the paralytic. Now I must go to the leper and seal my fate. **26.** Grief is seldom convenient to our scheduled worship.

27. I had a dear mentor, Constantinus, who was shepherd of the congregation in Antioch. His church's meeting house was near a busy road. One day, five minutes before his well-packed service was to begin, a Roman chariot ran over a beggar and left him dying before the church house. **28.** How grieved was the pastor that most of his members stepped over the bleeding man to carry their prayer scrolls on into the sanctuary.

29. Constantinus was a gentle pastor and full of the love of Christ. He scooped up the emaciated old man and carried him to his grieving widow. In the process of his ministry to this victim of Roman traffic, his hands and togas were fouled with blood. **30.** There was no time to go home and change clothes, so he entered his pulpit besmirched by the gore of his own compassion.

31. Clement, many in that congregation never forgave Constantinus his bloody toga. Ministry must ever be willing to face tradition. Somewhere a leper is dying. Tonight I shall act out a sermon. I can preach next week when human suffering is more remote.

THE SECOND LETTER OF EUSEBIUS OF PHILIPPI TO HIS BELOVED FRIEND, CLEMENT

1

A visit to the monastery of St. Thaddeus

1. A year has now passed since I wrote my last epistle to you. It has been a year of quiet for the church. We have not lost a single member to martyrdom, and we heard that the authorities were thinking of shipping the big cats to Rome where the persecution seems to be really getting under way. **2.** I cannot believe that in the economy of the kingdom God would rather have the cats eating Romans than Philippians. I can say the atmosphere here is not so tense, and we are breathing deeply.

3. I only wish I could say that I was feeling the same freedom in the assembly. For the last year Coriolanus has repeatedly explained to me God's will for my life. He believes I should leave this pulpit. **4.** He offered me a stipend of many shekels if I would take an empty pulpit just outside of Rome. I told him that I had heard that the Romans were receiving the Philippian lions to be ready for a new wave of per-

secution.   **5.** He informed me that a true man
of faith would never turn from lions to sidestep
the will of God in cowardly self-interest.

6. I am afraid, Most Excellent Clement, that
Coriolanus will not be content until I am no
longer shepherd of this flock.   **7.** Last week
he invited every elder of the church to his home
for squab and honey, but neglected to add me
to his invitation list. He is applying a kind of
ostracism.   **8.** It is possible to face it, but it
does keep me busy praying that I may not re-
ciprocate his hostility with hostility of my own.

9. I have learned a little more about the sad
care of one of my predecessors whom we have
called Tertius. It seems that on the day he entered the marketplace singing hymns he had
had a long discussion with Coriolanus who
explained to him the will of God.   **10.** According to Coriolanus it was the will of the Father
that Tertius join the order of St. Thaddeus. You
will recall that these monks live high on a rocky
pinnacle north of Atticus.   **11.** They all sub-
mit to having their tongues torn out so that
they never again will be tempted to utter a
single syllable that might break the silence of
their lifelong vigil of prayer.   **12.** While Tertius had always been known as a man of prayer,
the idea that his tongue would be tenderly re-
moved as a part of the sweet will of God had not
been revealed to him so clearly as it had been
revealed to Coriolanus.

13. Last week I visited the monastery at St. Thaddeus. It is all true. It is a silent settlement manned by thirty tongueless monks. But, my dear Clement, here was the startling impact of my discovery—twenty-two of them had once been the shepherds of local congregations before entering their tongueless lifestyles. **14.** Can you imagine that? I could but ponder what had taken those tongues once given to sermonizing and subjected them to amputation and the life of prayer and silence that it produced.

15. I must admit that mine was a silent sojourn among these brothers! They wheezed and breathed, occasionally sneezed, and I found out that many even snored, but year after year they passed without ever saying so much as "Good day!" **16.** Cicero Chrysostom and I became as good friends as we might with my talking and his nodding or writing monosyllable phrases on the scratch parchment.

17. Cicero had once preached in the suburbs of Philadelphia. By his own immodest testimony he was a popular preacher and large crowds attended him whenever and wherever he spoke the gospel. **18.** You are probably moving ahead of me in this tale, but he had his own Coriolanus who knew God's will for his life and, thus, the inner persecution began.

19. "Do you like the silent life?" I asked him.

20. He dipped his quill in the berry juice

and scratched on the parchment. "I like preach!" he wrote, living up to his monkish vows to write no more words than absolutely necessary to communicate what had to be said.

21. "How are the accommodations here?" I asked.

22. "Bed hard!" he wrote.

23. "And the food? Is it well prepared?" I asked.

24. "Bad cook! Food awful!" he complained with his quill and parchment.

25. "Do you miss preaching?" I asked.

26. Tears came to his eyes, and he dipped his quill and wrote for fully five minutes, "I like preach. I like feel God power. I like see people's faces when they hear sermon. I like power of spoken gospel.   **27.** I used to feel like God moved inside my life to form every word of sermon and people were powerless to resist. Once wrote sermon on repentance. Thirty-four Philippians heard sermon and came out of sin to Christ..."

28. He stopped writing. He buried his head in the sleeve of his robe and convulsed.

29. When he stopped convulsing, I spoke softly. "I am a preacher in Philippi, but I have been having second thoughts. I may come here and become your silent brother. You see, things aren't going well for me in the congregation, and I felt it may be God trying to tell me to..."

30. Cicero Chrysostom jumped up and shoved me onto the rough-carved bench. He dipped his quill into the ink and scrawled in large, angry letters across the parchment:

31. "NO! NO! NO! KEEP TONGUE! 'Faith comes by hearing and hearing by the word of God.' How shall they hear without a preacher?"

32. He stopped writing the giant letters and opened his mouth and faced me. There was an odd and powerless cavity. **33.** Nothing was behind his teeth, Clement. **34.** For the first time in my life I realized that silence cannot truly serve our dear Lord best. Only sound may serve. The sound must be trumpeted in faith. **35.** It must not quail before those who would seek to put to silence that speech of integrity that has something to say and has to say something... that sound that must trumpet a warning because it has seen the distant chasm and knows the pitfalls that the adversary has dug in the path of humankind.

36. Now I am back in Philippi. I am determined to preach the gospel.

37. Coriolanus may divert the flock from my affection, but he will not silence my tongue. **38.** It may be foolhardy to preach in the face of my current alienation, but by the foolishness of preaching I hope to fill my world with saving sound.

39. Clement, remember the monks of St. Thaddeus! Twenty-two of them would give their lives if they could just stand one more time in the marketplace and cry out above the hostile unbelievers, "Jesus Saves!"

2

The conversion of Croonus Swoonus

1. It is certain now that all of the lions are gone. The first wave of persecution is over, and we are enjoying a new period of peace and security. **2.** But security is never the friend of faith. It is peril that produces steadfastness. When the church is secure, she gains too many freedoms. She enjoys the freedom to doubt, the freedom to major on minor issues and the freedom to indulge herself in community acceptance.

3. The most ghastly freedom of all is the freedom from the utter dependency she must have to weather the crisis. Since the lions are gone, the people are speaking openly of being born again.

4. Even the mayor of Philippi is speaking unguardedly of being born again, and while these pagans have no idea what the term really means, they are sure that it has some connection with Christianity.

5. Others in our community are printing the words on their togas "Born Again" and "Try God." **6.** I tell you, Clement, it all started when they took the lions to Rome. You may be sure that when they bring them back there will be much less open talk and toga signs.

7. But now we are into it. It is almost a fad.

8. Some of the local actors are also saying that they have been born again. One of the tragedians in the local theater says he will never again do Greek tragedy, his joy is so great. **9.** He is going to become a joyous comedian and act in a thousand theaters to the joy of the Christ who has saved him. He is born again!

10. But the most notable conversion has been that of Croonus Swoonus. Yes, that is right; he, too, is born again. **11.** It all happened when his hairdresser who is a member of our church stuck a scripture parchment in his shining toga telling him how to be born again. And thus it happened.

12. He was famous before for his homespun ballads like "Back Homa in Roma" and "Nighty, Nighty, Aphrodity." But he is through crooning that he "found his thrill on Palatine Hill." **13.** Now he is born again, and he intends to give his entire life to singing songs in the traditions of the church. He has a stunning new composition called, "Pleeze Jesus, Just Seize Us and Heal Our Diseases."

14. Well, that is how it goes when one is born again.

15. How authentic Brother Swoonus is would be difficult to say. I know he means

well, but there were numerous rumors that his
singing career was about over when he had the
good fortune to be born again.   **16.** There is
something about his deportment that suggests
that the good fortune was really all God's and
that the Almighty was certainly lucky that the
golden throat once "given to the world" is now
"committed unto God."   **17.** I suppose it was
God's lucky day all right. At least the amphitheater is being packed night after night to hear
Croonus "lay 'em in the aisle for Jesus."

18. A single verse from his big-hit musical
testimony will tell you more than I can:

> I've been set completely free
> Since the man of Galilee
> Died upon the cross for me . . .
>   Yeah, Yeah, Yeah.

> Deaf and mute I had no sight.
> Life for me was just a fright,
> Till I stumbled into light . . .
>   Yeah, Yeah, Yeah.

> Now I'm giving up my sin,
> Love commandments one through ten,
> Praise the Lamb, I'm born again . . .
>   Yeah, Yeah, Yeah.

19. As you can see, Clement, this song is not
quite up to the one the beasts and elders sing

in the Apocalypse.

20. In the interest of Christian art it might be better to have the lions back. **21.** Pray for us that the faith that has such surface popularity may grow deep. Pray for Swoonus that his lyrics may improve even if his commitment does not.

3

Of the state of things in Philippi regarding Christian ministry, and why Eusebius felt it necessary to correspond with Clement at all

1. The Lord is faithful in a turbulent time when the very pinions of faith seem grounded. **2.** Much more in these days of joy have my thoughts been turned most naturally to you whose endurance is in a more southern pulpit.

3. Yes, to you, Clement, for while I have often heard you criticized by the brethren for your unconventional views, I still think that your own walk of faith is a triumph of honesty.

4. But let us consider our ministry in these latter days. **5.** Parchment is expensive, and I cannot write all I would about the degeneration of the faith. **6.** I am not overlooking the basic nature of Christianity. I know Christians are just people with their world view under renovation. **7.** But, beloved Clement, how shall the faith endure when there are so many blemishes on sanctity.

8. Do you remember when the emperor ordered the last purge? Some of those here in Philippi escaped arrest by joining the flight into the wilderness.   **9.** They went into the forest of Berea to win souls just as the authorities were locking up their less fortunate brothers who couldn't afford their timely excursions.   **10.** Are these wilderness witnesses for real? I believe not. They have found a way to minister that has alleviated all sense of personal risk.

11. Here, however, is born most of my reservations about a kind of faith that serves one's own safety before it serves His will.   **12.** I do not mean to be burdensome to our friendship, but I must ask if it is right for any preacher to build his own empire, replacing God's kingdom with his.   **13.** Many seem to determine God's will for their lives by first measuring exactly what each venture of faith will hold for themselves.   **14.** One of my most ardent members tells us that the one inviolable test for demonstrating whether something is the will of God or not is to say with openness, "This must be the will of God because it does so much for me."

15. There are many examples of this decaying Christian ministry in our day. I want to relate some primary examples and ask you to help me find a simple way to harmonize God's plan for His world and the attempt of so many Christians to use His purpose to further their own ends.

4

Christian ministry is always under threat by church business

1. There is something official and evil that always lurks around the board meetings of our church. **2.** When it is most blatant it disrupts the work of feeding the hungry or visiting the prisons. **3.** In fact, when our church's civil struggle gets fierce enough, all ministry comes to a stop.

4. You have, no doubt, heard by now of the fate of our most elect brother, Dubious, usually called Doob by the brethren in church. **5.** Doob has caused great consternation among his brothers because he has not been able to let his "yeas" be "yea" nor his "nays" be "nay." His "yeas" are usually "nay," and his "nays" are always "never." **6.** He wears a certain grieved look as though he has just discovered the gospel is bad news. He scowls over the communion cup and has a certain dyspeptic leer as though he had just won a dare with the Almighty.

7. Some say he wears his corset too tight,

and, hence, must live with his pinched expression. Others feel that he needs to mix his communion wine with the milk of human kindness. **8.** Some think it is essentially a liver problem.

9. At the last church conference, Doob slinked in, dragging his toga in defeat, and rose to make a motion that the youth of the church be censored for playing their lyricons in the meeting house. **10.** He denounced the "Boom-booms," the "Bangos," and the "Scotty-Wotty Jesus Four" as perverters of the great hymns of the church.

11. Elder Hector has a son in the "Scotty-Wotty Jesus Four," so in a moment there was a small explosion in the church meeting. **12.** Doob finally walked out only three votes short of stoning.

13. It was a terrible scene, my dear Clement. Doob is back on goat's milk to quiet his three-ulcered faith. **14.** The Elder Hector is trying to get the three necessary votes for Doob's stoning and the "Scotty-Wotty Jesus Four" say they are going to open their act in Ephesus where lyricons are welcome in the meeting houses.

15. I remember the words of our brother Paul who warned us that, if we bite and devour one another, we must be careful we are not consumed by one another. **16.** The quarrel itself is not the chief transgression but the good ministry that it replaces.

5

The marathon team

1. The times are free! Dear Clement, our church here at Philippi is fielding a marathon team which will participate in the Delphic Open Olympics. It is a five-man team of rugged, well-muscled men who in their preconversion lives were men of athletic reknown.

2. Each of them can run at least from Athens to Corinth and probably much farther. We are optimistic that they may, indeed, win this great set of games.

3. Last month Delos threw his discus with such force that the judges gasped at the record-setter, and were all the more amazed to find out he was a Christian.   **4.** He looks like Zeus and yet charges onto the field like an unbound Prometheus and immediately defeats all other discus throwers.

5. The times are free... free... FREE! Only a year ago we were afraid to go into the streets for fear of being arrested. Now we have our own athletic teams that are doing very well in the competition.   **6.** They are athletes who love the feel of pebbled track against their bare feet. They love the raw wind—the wafty air

of the Aegean Sea—full in their face. They love
the brisk air coming full against their nude
superiority as they fling the torch to the morning. They love the strain of their own competition set against the pagan athletes of the empire. **7.** They love all.

8. Perhaps not all. I am often concerned that
they may not love our dear Savior as much as
they love the game itself. **9.** They train for
months on end to have a go for the bronze
laurels of the games, but they are all too remiss
at training for the approval they may someday
need at the judgment seat of Christ. **10.** How
shall we build athletes who have learned the
secret of the life struggle against the tempter
himself?

11. We wrestle not against the wrestlers of
Smyrna and Thyatira. **12.** Do we seek the
laurel, display our trophy, claim our sweet victory, and never see Him who won His race in
the bleak light of Good Friday? **13.** Our
Christ entered the arena and wrestled with
principalities and powers and left to us that
same legacy. If there be a fault in the athletes
of our church, it is that they take their smaller
contests too seriously.

14. Menelaeus is our best miler. He rarely
makes church on Sunday morning since he
needs his sleep for his afternoon training ses-
sions. **15.** He rarely says grace before he
downs his yeast and beef. Of his own admis-

sion a great athlete is too busy on the track to spend much time studying the great scrolls of Scripture. **16.** But at least in the games he calls himself by the name "Christian," and having prayed for the laurel, he usually sees his prayer answered.

17. I found a certain athlete who declined to be a part of the church team. He was a slave of the emperor until he was made a free man only last year. **18.** He was called in the city of Rome the Italian Zephyr for he was a sprinter of so fleet a foot that it was said that none could match him. He was a snow courier. **19.** He ran snow from the top of the Apennines down to the palace so that Caesar could have his ice cream in late spring. He came to our church in the spirit of the victory that heralded his own vital walk with Christ.

20. When the other athletes were putting the team together just before the games at Athens, naturally they asked the Italian Zephyr to be a part of the team. He only sat and shook his head sadly. **21.** He would not join. He remembered his fellow slaves who had died in the dreadful attempt to bring the unthawed snow to the palace kitchen. For nothing more than a simple dish of ice cream for the Caesar, their own lives were forfeit.

22. "No," he said to those who sought to make him part of the team. "There is but one contest worth the running. There is but one

crown worth the struggle. There is but one
course that shall have my stamina."

23. "Which set of games? Which course?"
they persisted. "The track at Delphi or the stadium at Athens?"

24. Most of those who heard his answer
did not realize that he was quoting the letter
to the Hebrews, since most athletes are better
at running than reading, but the Italian Zephyr
simply lowered his eyes and told them of the
big race: **25.** "Wherefore seeing we also are
compassed about with so great a cloud of witnesses, let us lay aside every weight, and the
sin which doth so easily beset us, and let us
run with patience the race that is set before us,
Looking unto Jesus the author and finisher of
our faith; who for the joy that was set before
him endured the cross, despising the shame,
and is set down at the right hand of the throne
of God."

26. "Some race you just described," said
Menelaeus. "Who was the fellow that managed
that sort of marathon?"

27. 'If he lives here in Philippi," added
Delos, "let's get him on the team."

28. The Italian Zephyr shook his head.

29. After a moment he started to answer;
then he clutched his chest and died instantly.
The athletes looked on dumbfounded.

30. "He's dead!" said Menelaeus.

31. "Dead?" Delos was puzzled. "Athletes

don't die."

32. "Probably all those years of running snow to the palace," said Menelaeus checking his pulse and confirming the diagnosis.

33. "Probably," Delos nodded. "I wonder who that fellow was he was talking about who could run when the stands were filled with hecklers turning their thumbs down."

34. "I dunno," answered Menelaeus. "I'll tell you what, men. Let's get out there on the track and win this one for the old Zephyr."

35. And so they did!

6

*How ministry in the church
at Philippi is being destroyed by
theological controversy*

1. The church knows only two kinds of business. **2.** There is good business, which keeps the congregation pointed in the direction of ministry and looking out to its world.

3. There is bad business, which, congenial or not, diverts the church from its true course.

4. Our Savior himself once took the basin and towel and washed feet. **5.** How far we transgress when we slam the basin down, throw in the towel and stomp off in angry sandals!

6. But, Clement, theology too is sometimes

set against ministry. How I wish we might remember that Jesus was a practical rabbi. **7.** His compassion was such an urgent preoccupation with Him that he rarely took time to debate.

8. An incident happened in scroll study this week that will illustrate how far we have moved from Him who encourages us to give a cup of cold water in His name. **9.** Phoebe came to the women's scroll study with a most unusual question: "Will Jesus come before the great tribulation or after it?"

10. The question seemed innocent, but a great controversy soon broke out. **11.** Thirty-two women voted *pre* and thirty-two voted *post*.

12. In this ghastly deadlock Phoebe was undecided. She felt the uncomfortable strain of both groups wanting her to cast the deciding vote for their philosophy. **13.** She wanted more time to think about it. She was burdened, she said, by having the weight of our Lord's Second Coming fall squarely on her shoulders.

14. At this moment she is still undecided. She is studying furiously, realizing that so much of the planet's destiny rests on her decision. **15.** She thinks the recent destruction of the Jewish state by the hated Romans means that we have little time to get ready for the event. **16.** On the other hand, she feels that we are definitely in the last days, and she cannot tell if the great persecution now is the Great Tribulation or just one of the many inhumanities of man.

17. Some are saying that she is wishy-washy, and some say for the sake of harmony in the church she should make up her mind. One thing is sure: she is popular among all the women. **18.** After she casts the deciding vote, she will be popular with only half of them.

19. How dedicated are these who study? They meet every week to have dessert and discuss the end of the world. They show each other the latest interpretations of the scholars and bring their parchment charts on the final signs of the times.

20. I passed Phoebe late this afternoon on the way to the leper colony. I was surprised to see her not at the Second Coming scroll study which was anxiously awaiting her decision at that very time.

21. "Don't you care about the end of the world, Phoebe?" I asked.

22. "A little," she replied, "but I decided to go and help the lepers today."

23. "Alone?" I asked, for there was clearly no one with her.

24. "I must go alone," she said, "for there is so much need, and most of the women are at the Second Coming study."

25. "But what if they get the date all set and

your charts are unmarked?" I asked her.

26. She seemed not to hear. She was carrying a large basket of bandages for the lepers.

27. I couldn't bear to see her carrying such a large basket alone. I took the basket from her and walked along with her.

28. We walked in silence toward the leprosarium. I could not repress a kind jibe. "Phoebe," I blurted out. "Don't you care? Is our Lord coming back before or after the tribulation? When he comes back, where do you want to be found—in this state of indecision or at the Second Coming study?"

29. "There is where I want to be found," she said, pointing to a circle of low, thatched huts.

30. A little boy came running up to us from the compound. His face was badly blighted and part of his hand was gone.

31. "When do you think the Lord is coming back, my child?" asked Phoebe. A single tear ran down across his cheek.

32. I handed her a bandage and couldn't remember why I thought the question was so important.

33. I can tell you this, Clement, I did not find among all the lepers a single chart of these dreadful last days.   **34.** It was as if the lepers had lost interest in the whole issue of the Second Coming.   **35.** We spent the afternoon binding lesions.

7

*How worship in the city of
Philippi interrupted the
church's ministry*

1. I have long believed that worship is the business of the church collected. 2. Adoration and praise is important among all of God's people. 3. I have also believed that it should be done creatively. 4. Too often the worship of the church just happens; it isn't well planned.

5. Boredom in the church is the evidence that neither sermons nor worship services have been well planned. 6. Remember Eutychus who fell asleep during Paul's sermon and fell out the window? 7. Could planning worship save nodding slaves from broken necks?

8. Our problem is different. Services here at Philippi suffer from too much planning. They are a production. 9. Those who worship here are leaving the service with great applause for the actors, almost demanding encores. 10. But who remembers Him in whose honor we are gathered?

11. And it is the planning itself that stirs up dissension. 12. Consider our annual Easter pageant, a remarkable performance on our Lord's resurrection. You may have seen it—it is

always a cold show with frost on the sepulcher.

13. One of the deacons stands behind a clump of bushes at sunrise and reads the scroll while Mary Magdalene approaches, weeping her way up to the grave. **14.** Then a deep voice thunders out above the tomb, "Weep not, Maria. He is not here for He is risen!"

15. At this point the choir, which has been shivering in the Easter air booms out the anthem, "No Room in the Tomb for Gloom." **16.** Then everyone shakes hands and hurries to the Hall of Tyrannus to have hot nectar and resurrection bread.

17. Last year there was a great crowd, the annuciation angel appeared with his trumpet on schedule, but the director was horrified that he was wearing a turban to cover his ears. An angel in a turban?

18. Now the church is locked in a great controversy whether or not angels should be allowed to wear fleeces and shawls, and most of all, whether the annunciation role should be given to anyone who had disturbed the performance last year. **19.** Two people have already quit the choir, and the actors are incensed by the criticism. **20.** Sister Syntyche says she will not come back to the tomb until someone makes apologies to her dear friend, Erastus, who played the resurrection angel.

21. Never since our dear Savior walked out of the tomb has His resurrection caused such a stir.   **22.** Should not we, Brother Clement, emphasize the life of the church as that dear, kind quality of life that our Savior brought back from the grave? There is something anti-Christ about an Easter quarrel!

23. Sentrus the Seer says that this is to be another cold resurrection morning.   **24.** The Oracle at Delphi agrees that Michael could be back in a turban. What's a poor resurrection angel to do with such a frigid forecast?

25. If you should see a red glow in the northern sky on Easter morning, you will know that a quarrel in Philippi has erupted and that Easter has finally destroyed what it was born to create.

26. And once again the ministry of the church will have ceased while we quarrel over the Prince of Peace.

8

The Berean Wagon Ministry and its shortcomings

1. Hylus, the pastor of the church in Berea, is trying to get me to begin a new children's ministry which he says will double the attendance at our children's service.   **2.** Berea began the ministry only last month, and they have had unparalleled success.   **3.** I have been resisting the pressure in our little congre-

gation to begin a wagon ministry here in Philippi. **4.** Is the competition of nearby congregations to build the biggest attendance at
scroll study an exercise in one-up-manship?
5. Here is how it works. **6.** On the Lord's
Day a huge harvest wagon travels out the
Athenian Way as far as West Berea. It picks up
children and brings them back to scroll study
in Berea. **7.** Last month thirty-three *puellae*
and thirty-four *pueri* rode the wagon. Each of
the children received a cluster of grapes and
a little squab just for riding the wagon to
church.

8. It worked so well that a second wagon is
being sent to the neighborhoods at East Berea
this Sunday, and this week every child who
brings an *amicus* gets an autographed parchment from Evangelist Octavius. **9.** Every
child who brings more than ten *amici* gets a
hub bolt from a Roman chariot. **10.** They are
expecting more than a hundred children in the
wagon ministry this week. **11.** The pastor
told me that if it works they plan to tape a lucky
denarius under the wagon box for the child
who brings the most *amici*.

12. I have heard of a church south of Athens
that has twenty-seven wagons in their ministry now, and the adult winner of last month's
contest got an all-expense-paid trip to Antioch.
13. They had a motto: Believe in the Rock, and
go to Antioch. The winning child received an

equus minimus. They had over four hundred in scroll study.

14. The future of wagon ministry, however, may not be bright. Many of the Romans, it is believed, are only letting their children ride the wagons to get them out of the atrium for a quiet Sunday morning.

15. Rumor says the Christians and the lions may soon be at it again. Probably the Romans will keep their children in till the season of hate is over. **16.** It can be dangerous to be baptized during the games, and most Romans will not run the risk of letting their children get on a church wagon for fear they may get thrown to the lions.

17. Clement, I must be honest; I am afraid we may communicate an easy gospel where children come to church only for squab and grapes. **18.** There has been some disaster in the church. Some of the older members in Berea said that the little Romans are sticky and greasy, and they leave the wagons full of seeds and bones.

19. I suppose if children are led to know Christ, there is some merit to the ministry, but does it not create wagon-ride Christians? **20.** Is there a way to win children without spending so much money on squabs and grapes? **21.** Wouldn't our Lord, who consistently taught self-denial, see this as evangelism by indulgence? **22.** I could use a restful week in Antioch, but I think I will pay my own way.

23. It is so hard to know how our Lord would have us minister to children. I remember the tender picture of Him cuddling them in His arms and telling the quarreling apostles that the kingdom would be composed of the child-like. **24.** I just can't picture Him loading them in wagons and giving them prizes.

9

The abominable monster of Bythinia

1. Are young people in Coos dropping out of church? **2.** The pastors in this area aren't sure what to make of it. **3.** Some feel that the youth are not seeing credible Christian elders in the church. **4.** I call to witness Hezekiah, the abominable monster of Bythinia.

5. Hezekiah was found wandering in the forests of Cenchrea. **6.** It would be impossible to tell you all of my impressions of this young man, although I might describe for you his symptoms. **7.** He is stooped and haggard far beyond his years. He is unshaven. He prefers sitting quietly in a corner and ignoring the world. **8.** Ever and anon he will pick up a scripture scroll and growl and begin chewing on it.

9 When I first saw him growling and chewing, I thought that he must be an incorrigible youth who had spent a great deal of his life chewing on sacred scripture. **10.** We all know some worldly-wise young man who cannot bear to be told anything, "lest having eyes he see, and having ears he hear."

11. But this proved to be a false assumption. He came into the assembly growling and chewing and making a frightful noise while the rest of us tried in vain to sing the psalms of which we have grown so fond. **12.** During the singing of "Blest Be the Bonds of Jesus' Love" his growling became ever more intense. **13.** And when a brother prayed for the "sweet, sweet fellowship" of the church, he nearly gnawed the spindle from the scroll.

14. It was only yesterday that I learned the truth about poor, mad Hezekiah. He was at the business meeting in the congregation in Cenchrea where a brother was dismissed for his views on baptism. **15.** Well, there was a very narrow vote to release him—some feeling his views were sound and others feeling his views were *only* sound. **16.** A quarrel broke loose and half the congregation led by True-to-the-Word Marcus promptly denounced those who had denounced the brother and left the meeting hall. **17.** A third group denounced everyone, having already taken a stand against denunciations in the church.

18. Hezekiah is an impressionable young man, and he had only recently become a disciple. **19.** He became distraught, not knowing whether to follow the major position, the minor position or the antidenunciationists. **20.** It put such a strain on his own need to be secure he began weeping and then, of course, chewing scrolls.

21. I have seen one other case. This young person on seeing Christians set against each other went off to study philosophy in Athens. I regret to say he has become an atheist lecturer and is trying to get "In Deus We Trust" taken off every last denarius in circulation.

22. Oh, the harm that is done when our convictions supersede our compassion! **23.** It is especially the young who suffer. They can't seem to love Jesus and a fighting church at the same time. **24.** Did not our brother Paul encourage us to "be kind one to another, tenderhearted, forgiving one another, even as God for Christ's sake has forgiven us"? It is certainly spiritual wisdom.

25. It looks as though we may have to put poor Hezekiah in chains lest he chew more scrolls than he has the stomach to digest. **26.** I cannot say his madness is terminal. **27.** I am told there is a certain hairy creature in the outer forests of Galatia who lurks outside empty churches on the dark of the moon and pounces on old elders as they wind past their empty meeting halls. **28.** Some say the Ghoul of Galatia is a wolf who once wore sheep's clothing until he saw the sheep devouring each other. **29.** They are trying to trap him now, but I have the feeling that when they do they will only have discovered a night fiend created in a vicious church business meeting.

30. Clement, you see why it is so important for me to accompany Phoebe when she goes to the leper colony. **31.** There is a leper there named Simon. He cannot live much longer, but he has a rich baritone voice that will be with him to the last of his life. **32.** I heard him singing the ninetieth psalm the other day, and I knew again how important it was that each of us number our days, and thus, apply our hearts unto wisdom.

33. I remember that the psalmist also said, "He that winneth souls is wise." Our Lord once drove the moneychangers from the temple. **34.** Perhaps He did it so that the temple would not be the place where men use God's good ground to grow their own rank reputations. **35.** Temples create either monsters or ministers. **36.** May Christ so tower above our assemblies that we shall meet only to worship God and to roll bandages for the broken world.

10

The return of the lions

1. Three crates of lions were unloaded today at the seaport of Neapolis. In our prayer group this afternoon one of our members prayed that they were for the city zoo.   **2.** But on the way home from church I saw the great cages being towed along the causeway to the stadium. **3.** Clement, we are very much in for it, I fear.

4. I was one of the four men who helped carry Publius the Paralytic home after our prayer meeting.

5. "Have you ever been in prison for the faith?" I asked Publius.

6. "No," he laughed, "and I never will be!"

7. "Why? How can you be so certain?" I asked.

8. "What jailer wants to be bothered with a paralytic? Only Christians can tolerate such creatures as myself. No pagan jailer wants to be bothered with someone who requires bed-pans and spoon-feeding.   **9.** I couldn't commit a crime had I the will to. And it would have to be a magnificent crime before any jailor would lock me up."

10. "You're jailproof," laughed one of the other litter carriers.

11. We joined him in laughter before we all turned the corner, and were suddenly brought face to face with the caged beasts that had just been unloaded. Their size caused each of us to shudder as we passed. **12.** We tried not to imagine the confrontation that might be ours if the persecution does indeed come.

13. We had walked a mile before any of us could break the silence. I finally spoke, "What would you do, Publius, if you were thrown to the lions?"

14. "Do?" he answered with a weak chuckle. "What do paralytics always 'do'? The only thing I could do would be to spit in his eye. It wouldn't be much of a defense. **15.** 'Do'? I'd just lie there and try to taste as bad as I possibly could."

16. We laughed at the thought of it. **17.** "Perhaps we should start praying that God would make every Christian in Philippi taste so bad that no beast of wholesome palate would ever consider us tasty," said a man on the other side of the litter as he changed hands on the stretcher pole.

18. "Still," said Publius, "they never throw paralytics to the lions. There's no show in that for these overfed Romans. **19.** Think how you'd feel if you had paid thirty shekels for a season ticket to watch Christians scream and run and then be forced to watch them eaten, immobile and paralyzed. Why, you would de-

mand your money back and reinvest it in
Gladiatorial Combat. **20.** So far they have yet
to throw one paralytic to the lions. I've checked
the casualty lists in all the arenas. They don't
even throw in the seriously crippled. **21.** Take
it from me, if you want to be lionproof when
the heat is on, you just get a good friend to de-
tach your spinal cord at the thirteenth vertebra
and you'll be safe forever. Still, you'd best be
sure that you've got four fine Christians such
as yourselves who'll carry you to services the
rest of your life."

22. Soon we arrived at Publius' hut and de-
posited him safely inside.

23. "Publius, have you prayed for healing?"
asked one of the men.

24. "I once prayed for nothing else," he replied, "but only my head continued to move
to exert my will. I have cried myself to sleep
many nights. **25.** I do not even have the muscles which would give my mind enough obe-
dience to commit suicide. But I will one day
meet the Master just beyond the threshold of
death. Then you who have carried me to a
thousand prayer meetings will see me spring
upright, and I shall leap in the healing light of
heaven . . . I will dance . . . and run a thousand
tireless furlongs. **26.** Sometimes I cannot tell
if first I would like to see Jesus and then run and
leap or to run and leap and then see Jesus. But
my agenda for heaven is as simple as these two

items."

27. "But what of the future? Do you not fear it?" asked another.

28. "No, for in the future I shall meet God. It is the *now* that seems most wearisome. I have presumed upon your eight good arms and legs to keep my dead frame from taking root. Oh, dear brothers, you must face the lions. I must face only my daily unwillingness to be a burden to the church of Christ. **29.** I am confident that you will tend to me until the threshold of eternity. **30.** The first lion I must face is the lion of Judah, and I shall be free to run the golden fields with the lion of St. Mark. Forgive my heavy, dead existence until that day shall dawn."

31. A tear crossed his cheek.

32. In the distance we heard the lions roar.

33. We all knew that there was shortly to be an edict that might affect the entire life of the church—perhaps its very existence.

34. Still, we all felt a kind of victory in the presence of a man who did not have to fear lions. Even so we didn't really want to pray.

35. I took a flask of wine and poured the contents into five cups. We broke a loaf of bread and passed the pieces to the others in the small hut.

36. "This is His body!" said Publius as I held the bread to his mouth and he ate.

37. "This is His blood—the blood of the new

covenant, in force beyond the threshold," I said as I held my small tin cup to his lips.

38. Again we heard across the silent night the roaring beasts. One of the men held his cup toward the ceiling.

39. "To the great lion," he said, "the lion of Judah, the lion of St. Mark." We all brought our cups together in the thin clanging that tin can make on tin. We drank.

"This is the blood of the New Testament!" said Publius.

40. We smiled at the distant roaring.

THE
THIRD
LETTER
OF
EUSEBIUS
OF
PHILIPPI
TO HIS
BELOVED
FRIEND,
CLEMENT

1
Mock cheer

1. I am in prison.

2. Coriolanus is still free, and he came to my cell today to bring greetings from the flock. I have been concerned about their welfare in my absence, so his visit was welcome. **3.** But there was little cheer in his cheer. As a matter of fact, his cheer left me depressed for five hours.

4. He feels that it would be a glorious honor for me to be thrown to the lions should my imprisonment end in the den. Oh, Clement, that is easy for him to say! **5.** One should not turn from glory or take it lightly. But the prospect of my martyrdom did not afford me the honest joy that it supplied him. **6.** Then he asked me if I would let him have my tunic if my name became posted for the honor of this ultimate witness. "No use getting it all torn and spotted," he said. "We must be practical. . . . A good tunic is hard to come by these days."

7. "How about my sandals?" I asked, with much less buoyance than characterized his attitude.

8. "Do you mind going barefoot?" he asked.

9. "The afternoon sand can be awfully hot," I replied.

10. "But not for long," he said, "and some of our flock would appreciate your kindness at the hour of such a gallant and selfless witness. It would be a glorious example to the whole church."

11. "Well, I'm all for exemplary living... or dying," I said.   **12.** I was eager to change the subject. "Maybe I'll be released."

13. "Don't count on it," he counseled. "Just keep your eyes on Jesus!"

14. "All right," I said, "but if I am released I can hardly wait to get back to the assembly and preach again."

15. "Well, I don't know if you should go directly to the church from prison. Many of our people don't like the idea of having an ex-convict in the pulpit."

16. "I see."

17. "It doesn't set a good example for the children. I must be honest, Brother Eusebius, you've lost a lot of credibility with the flock. **18.** While we don't want you to become discouraged and we wish you Christian cheer, it has come to our attention that there is a little chapel in Konos that needs a new pastor."

19. "But Konos is nearly a ghost town!"

20. "Ah, but God loves those people..."

21. "What people?"

22. "The people of Konos. There are a few people in that congregation, and God loves them just as much as he loves those of Philippi. To minister to the few is as important as to the many."

23. I meditated a good long time. Just as Coriolanus was standing to leave, I finally asked the question, "So it is either the lions or the pulpit at Konos?"

24. He nodded his head and smiled.

25. "Be of good cheer and look to Jesus!"

26. After he left I found myself even more morose than before. How am I to pray, my dear Clement? Should one desire to be devoured or to pastor in a ghost town?   **27.** I am riddled by resentment. How can I be charitable and cheerful thinking about being devoured while Coriolanus wears my robe and sandals to my execution?   **28.** It is death or the dust of Konos, I suppose.   **29.** More than my uncertain future, I am troubled about the cheer I received from Coriolanus.   **30.** Such Christians make lions look kind.

31. They say our brother from Atticus had such a deacon. The day he was to be devoured, his adversary came to observe. I can barely stand the idea that Coriolanus might be there on my fateful day should it come.   **32.** I am frozen by the cold image of a deacon grinning above my martyrdom and cheering the beasts.

33. Compassion is of Christ. A Christian with mock cheer is probably a mock Christian. And those who grin at martyrs must be like those who once thronged the cross with dice and vinegar. **34.** I once heard there was a Pharisee who stood in the Good Friday crowd. While our Lord cried, "Eloi, Eloi, lama sabachthani?" he was crunching bread and pomegranates. It is a bleak heart that packs sandwiches for crucifixions. **35.** Animosity cloaked in piety is a demon even if it sits in church praising the Creator.

36. Oh, I am alone. "Eloi, Eloi, lama sabachthani?"

2

The encroachment of Mt. Olympus

1. Clement, time drags slowly in a cell. The days are drudgerous. "Tempus fugit" is a lie. I have filled up some of the empty hours by a new concern about syncretism.

2. I am increasingly disturbed that Romans seem to be quite subtle in blending their worship of Zeus with our own immortal Jehovah. **3.** I hope you will tell me that I am being oversensitive. Generations yet unborn will suffer

unless we recognize the possibilities of syncretism. **4.** Those who are converted to
Christianity from their pagan shrines often
come into our fellowship wagging their poly-
theism behind them.

5. Take their enthusiasm for Vesta, the goddess of home. We have actually had a sugges-
tion that we in the Christian church try to
adopt a hearth emphasis. **6.** They do not
want to call it the day of the Vestal Virgins, only
Mater Dies. Should we have a mother's day?
7. There does seem to be something noble in
the idea, but buried in it is the idea of Vesta,
goddess of the hearth.

8. Clement, I know you're an orphan, so
you may not understand this desire to start a
day when all families who love our dear Lord
will be able to honor their mothers as well.

9. So there you are, Clement—Mater's Day!
On such a day we could honor our mothers and
write poems about them, pin roses on their
togas and generally do nice things for them.

10. I mentioned the idea to Publius the
Paralytic who was brought to the jail yesterday
to visit us, but he was not enthusiastic either.
"Sheer syncretism," he said. **11.** "What
about all the mothers who practice infanticide
or abortion?" he queried. **12.** "What will
they wear on their togas? A thistle or a spray of
thorns? And what about Cressia the Creepie,
who burned her poor babies with faggots just

to hear them scream!" Publius became as ani-
mated as his paralysis would allow.   **13.** "Yes,
Eusebius, what about these child abusers...
Mater Horribilis? What shall they wear on their
togas?

14. "Besides, you start to honor them, and
they'll form groups and clubs and soon they'll
want to vote in the proconsul elections!   **15.**
Then you'll have anarchy.   **16.** Mark my word,
Eusebius, give a *mater* one pace and she'll take
a furlong! They might even form groups that
will say that if a *mater* does the work of a *pater*,
she should get the same pay.   **17.** That could
erode confidence in the denarius. Then you'll
have inflation and a storm of liberated *maters*
marching on Rome; it'll make Spartacus look
like Via Sesemia.   **18.** Before you know it
they'll be calling snowmen 'snowpersons,' and
girls will be training as gladiators.

19. "Is that what you want—women teaching in the church and men washing dishes?
Legionnettes, not legionnaires? Equal rights
for *feminae?*   **20.** Then some radical *mater* will
stand in the forum and pray to her 'Mother in
Heaven,' and it will all be over.   **21.** If they
pin roses on their togas, it could change the
whole sexual philosophy of *Roma* itself!"

22. By this time Publius the Paralytic was so
excited by the power of his own oratory I
thought that he might jump up at any moment.

23. "No, by heaven. I'll not pin a flower for the reign of feminine terror and oppression it might spur." **24.** After he was gone, I thought of the priority most people placed on motherhood.

25. I suppose it does have its risks, but I think I may go ahead and try to get *Mater's Day* going. What can it hurt? It's not for Vesta but for Jesus. **27.** Here's to roses on togas.

3

More on the fear of syncretism

1. I can endorse *Mater's Day* more easily than the new emphasis on romance. **2.** I'm speaking of Valentinus. While he is not Bishop of Philippi, the accusation against him could bring trouble for all of us. **3.** And to what end are his romantic notions?

4. Valentinus wants to see the institution of Christian marriage. This is in direct contradiction to the Roman civil law. **5.** Who knows where this whole thing might lead? **6.** It is exactly in this way that traditions begin. **7.** Right now unless he burns incense to the the Emperor, he is slated to be shot by archers.

8. Some in the church are saying that Val has his values scrambled, that he has unwitingly confused Cupid with Christ. **9.** Some say he was ever the romanticist humming "Hearts and Flowers" when he should have been studying the book of Romans or helping his church understand the perplexing issues of the Second Coming.

10. In truth, Clement, there is not one biblical text in support of his madness. Our dear Lord never once taught that people should be married by the Book.   **11.** Nor is there a single injunction in the letters of Paul that teach what Valentinus calls the "Christian Marriage."

12. The bishops disagree with one another, but all of them are asking, "Where will it all end?"   **13.** During these ceremonies Val's disciples are standing up before young brides and grooms and "calling down Cupid."   **14.** They say, "Beloved in Christ, we gather here and these two people come to pledge their love."   **15.** Then they sing, if you please, various sorts of romantic ditties, light candles and kiss right in the house of God! On the mouth, too!   **16.** Mind you, I'm open to new ideas, but I think Valentinus may have gone too far. If you start with Christian marriages, someone could suggest Christian prayer in the Roman Senate and invocations at athletic events. **17.** You could actually develop a whole lifestyle under the name of Christ.

18. I'm insecure. I think we should keep Christ for the Christians and Cupid for the Olympians. Pastor Valentinus is sure to be executed by the archers, and who for? **19.** He will be the first martyr to have lived for Christ and be shot for Cupid.

20. There are too many new ideas bombarding the church at once. Pray for me, Clement, that I can handle them all with some sense of balance. **21.** In prison the issues are more difficult to understand than they might be if I were free.

22. I am bewildered. Think of the mess the world will be in with everybody falling in love and sending each other poetry.

4

Concern about the Festival of Demons

1. Here in the north of Greece we have a custom that has grown increasingly more popular.

2. It must have come originally from Circe the Sorceress. **3.** Lamentably, the custom celebrates the realm our Lord so much abhorred: the kingdom of the demons. **4.** Ordinarily if one finds a demon on his doorstep he drives it out or calls for the village exorcist. **5.** But at this autumn festival of the damned we actually celebrate the dark kingdom. **6.** Since you do not have this custom in the South, you may find the idea untenable. **7.** But here we are celebrants at this festival. **8.** The day is almost here. **9.** Soon the little ones will be tripping the streets of Philippi dressed as goblins and crying out at every door for sweetmeats.

10. These little village demons are too much like ourselves. We are at once ugly and beautiful, holy and sinister, good and ghoulish. How shall we ever learn to deal with the two sides of our nature? **11.** How often, my dear Clement, have I wished vengeance on people who mistreated me. **12.** The children are like us in one other way. They hide behind faces that are not theirs. **13.** Ah, that we might take away our demon faces and let our real countenance shine through. **14.** But alas, it is easier to wear a mask. An ugly face is sometimes better than a real one. Thus are we afraid to show each other who we really are. **15.** All of us endure the goblinhood that masks our fear of being known.

16. Those who wear a pretense sometimes end up all that they pretend. **17.** Has all our bloody history come from faces molded by the masks they wore? **18.** Dear Christ, make one that which we are and that which we appear to be. Be Lord of naked faces.

5
How traditions get started

1. I have had the feeling that traditions are often the result of happenstance and sentimentality. We must be careful. Have you heard of the Figgy Ghost? **2.** He passes through the city every night, and those children who have lost a tooth may put it on the window ledge and he will pass in the darkness and exchange the tooth for a fig.

3. The myth is perpetuated by the parents who teach it to their children and do themselves the work they attribute to the Figgy Ghost. **4.** What in the name of Pluto would the ghost want with a million Greek teeth? Where would he keep them? How much of the poor ghost's life is dedicated to fig picking? Where does a pure spirit find the muscles to lug around a basket of goodies and teeth?

5. Behind traditions are the ashes of logic.

6. Some say it all began in a tale of Aesop several centuries ago. Some say the old Greek storyteller himself is the Figgy Ghost, leaving his grave every night to delight the Aegeans. **7.** But it likely all started when the governor's wife realized that a fig was good for the healing of her children's gums, or when a clever cook lost a tooth in a green fig and contrived the story for the procurator's children.

8. But I am most worried about some of the Christian traditions I have observed getting started. For the last two years we have had Sandal-Egging. **9.** Phoebe detests the tradition and despises the notion that she herself started this one because she lent two eggs to her neighbor.

10. Can she be blamed? Ah, Clement, no one loves Christ or despises shallow traditions more than Pheobe, but she did lend her neighbor eggs. **11.** And as luck would have it, when her neighbor came to return the eggs, Phoebe wasn't home. The neighbor noticed that Phoebe had hung her sandals on a branch to dry after she had washed them. **12.** Without thinking, Phoebe's friend just put the eggs in the toe of the sandals and went home.

13. When Phoebe returned, she was hungry and couldn't find a thing in the house to eat. Our economy being what it is, she didn't have even a single denarius to go to market. So she decided to go on a prayer fast.

14. After she had finished fasting and praying that God might provide something for her to eat, she went out to the branch to retrieve her sandals and, lo, she discovered the eggs. **15.** She was so struck by the eggs that she fell down before the bush and thanked our God for the miracle. Then she looked at the particular bush on which she had hung her sandals. It was a sandalwood tree.

16. The leaves of the sandalwood shrub are egg-shaped with a tiny crossvein in the center of the leaf.   **17.** As Phoebe thought about the miracle of the *ova* and she saw the little crosses in the center of the leaves, she could not help but think of Christ and His sacrifice.

18. She shared the experience with the Women's Scroll Fellowship. Some were so moved that they wept. Thus the sandal-egging tradition was born.   **19.** For the last two years the women of Philippi have decorated their homes with boughs of sandalwood and left eggs in the toes of each other's sandals to represent the message of the cross and the fertility of the gospel among the heathen.

20. It sounds absurd. But the custom is spreading and some churches in the remotest provinces are celebrating the miracle by the customs I have just suggested. Clement, be careful where you hang your toga or your sandals or your tunic.   **21.** Human sentiment issues from a sweet insanity that can build a lovely idea from things base.   **22.** If we continue to clutter the simplicity of the gospel, we could lose its power altogether.

23. Phoebe feels responsible for this digression. She said during the season just past she could not find a single woman in Philippi who would come to scroll study. They all had to do some last-minute shopping for eggs or new sandals or they were off to the woods to collect boughs of sandalwood.

24. She confessed her grief to me. "Eggs are better scrambled than worshiped. Sandals are better worn than adored," she said. "Could I borrow your axe?" she asked me. **25.** "Sure," I said, "but why?"

26. "I'm going home to cut down my sandalwood shrub."

27. "It's no use, Phoebe. You can't call back a tradition once you create it."

28. "Not even if I hang my sandals inside to dry from now on?"

29. "It is too late. Straight thinking is the only way to combat the sentimentality that smothers truth in heaping sweetness."

30. Clement, it is here that honesty is saved. We cannot chop down the shrines of sentiment, but we do not have to stop and worship. **31.** Pray for Phoebe. Imagine how you would feel if sandal-egging were laid at your feet.

32. Traditions must be strangled as infants.

33. They say over in Berea that last Lord's Day a surprised child found a new toy in his father's leggings. There was also a note that the toy was given to help the child remember that the holy wise men once gave presents to the baby Jesus. **34.** It could be nothing, but we had better keep our eye on this one.

6

Of rules and freedom

1. Brother James came to my cell today. He wanted my counsel on holding the annual Cupid Banquet in the Hall of Bacchus. **2.** I felt there were several things wrong with the idea. First, the persecution being what it is, if a careless young Christian drew a fish on the washroom walls, our entire youth department could be incarcerated. **3.** But there was a more immediate consideration for the church.

4. Coriolanus and the elder Scrubjoy believe that it is impossible for a Christian to drink and go to heaven. Not that there would be any of that at the dinner, but its mere association with the sinful Hall of Bacchus leaves the whole event in question. **5.** Do we not all know that the Hall of Bacchus in Philippi is the epicenter of all debauchery in Northern Greece?

6. Brother James does occasionally take a little wine for his frequent infirmity, and Coriolanus strongly disapproves. **7.** Scrubjoy went so far as to say that his infirmities would be less frequent if his tippling were less frequent.

8. Brother James is in for trouble. **9.** Scrubjoy was once the chief customer at the Hall of

Bacchus, staggering home night after night. One night his bleary eyes misled him and he stumbled into the back of our church entirely by mistake. **10.** Flavius the Flame was holding special services, and at the conclusion, Scrubjoy swaggered forward and laid his flask on the altar. **11.** He came to love our Lord as much as he hated the "filthy, dirty, rotten liquor," as he put it.

12. He constantly told the youth to stay away from all appearance of evil. He warned them about compromising their convictions. **13.** "You cannot serve God and Bacchus," he used to say. "You will never find drinking lips and praying tongue in the same mouth, just as you will never find a dancing foot and a praying knee on the same leg."

14. Yes, Clement, Scrubjoy became incensed when he heard of a church member having a drink or going to a dance. And whenever he heard that anyone both danced and drank, he would move to the other side of the street and trace the sign of the cross in the air.

15. Gradually Scrubjoy came to emphasize personal purity as the ideal of the believer. **16.** Under his spell many in the church have become disciples by "notting." **17.** If you do *not* drink and you do *not* dance and you do *not* leer at the hemlines of short tunics, then you may go to heaven where presumably everybody will get together for celebrating an eternity of Scrubjoy's discipline.

18. So Brother James has agreed not to hold the dinner in the Hall of Bacchus. They can all have a picnic in the park and have just as good a time. **19.** He could remember when Brother Timothy came to our church to lecture on Christian sexuality. Scrubjoy rose erect and dry and scowled at the congregation.

20. "Christian sexuality, my brothers, for shame! Did not our Lord tell us that we are to have His mind? **21.** Should the church ever focus on smut and bless it with the name of Christian? We must take a stand against this wicked doctrine," he cried.

22. Several older brothers shouted, "Amen!"

23. "You will never find drinking lips and a praying tongue in the same mouth! You will never find a dancing foot and a praying knee on the same leg! And my brothers and sisters, you will never find Christian thoughts and a lusty mind in the same brain!" cried Scrubjoy.

24. "Amen!" cried the others.

25. Scrubjoy is, indeed, keeping himself unspotted from the world and his countenance is stern. **26.** Clement, it is not God's commandments but our own that become so grievous. We make the world miserable in measuring each other by our own moral maxims. **27.** The youth of Philippi are tired of being inspected for such blemishes as Scrubjoy delights to find.

28. Rules blunt the appetite for Christ.

29. Joy intrigues.

30. I can tell you it has been many a season since Scrubjoy has bubbled anyone into the kingdom.

31. One Saturday night they threw into my cell Cassius the Crock. He reeked of brew so strongly that the rats all left, but by morning his stupor had thawed.   **32.** Who can admire his habit? Still, it has blessed him with a sort of wisdom.   **33.** He was in no immediate danger. They don't throw drunks to the lions, only Christians. He knew he'd be out by noon. When he found out that I had already been in prison for all these months, he looked downcast.

34. "I used to have a good drinking pal who became a Christian," he said. "A fellow named Scrubjoy, the riot of the ale halls. Ever hear of him?"

35. "Maybe," I said cautiously.

36. "Well, he was one funny man. We used to laugh and sing half the night. He knew more funny stories than the god of wine himself. But he became a Christian and I haven't seen him smile since.   **37.** Tell me, Reverend, why would a man want to believe in Christ so much that he'd be willing to give up smiling and risk the lions, too?"

38. "Hmm!" I said as the jailor came. He took the keys and gestured to Cassius and unlocked the door.

39. Cassius staggered upward, still talking. "You see, Reverend, drunks get out on Sunday and they have a lot better time than Christians. You sure you don't know Scrubjoy?"

40. "Maybe," I repeated.

41. "Well, it wouldn't do any good to throw Scrubjoy to the lions. Even the beasts aren't all that anxious to devour a bland life," he said.

42. He started out the door, then turned back for a last comment. "I'll tell you this. You'll never find a happy man and a Christian in the same tunic."

43. The door clanged shut.

7

Praise and earthquakes

1. Coriolanus has been arrested and has now become my cell mate. At first I protested to God that there was no justice in the universe. Coriolanus now and my own possible martyrdom in the future! Gradually I am adjusting.

2. We have lived together without resentment. **3.** Tuesday night Coriolanus made a magnificent discovery. Near the base of the wall he found the Latin names Paul and Silas etched in the stone at the end of a prayer. **4.** We noticed that the cell wall was crossed by fissures that could have been caused by a great earthquake. **5.** Suddenly it dawned on us that perhaps this was the very cell where the Apostle Paul was once a prisoner.

6. Remembering how Paul and Silas sang at midnight as God sent an earthquake to open the doors of the jail, we took courage. **7.** "Do it again, God!" cried Coriolanus near midnight. He began to sing a hymn in monotone, and I joined in. We praised God at full volume with some of the great songs of the faith. **8.** Ever and anon we stopped to see if we could hear even the faintest rumblings of a quake. By three in the morning we still had not raised a tremor and decided to give it up. There seemed so little to rejoice about. **9.** Suddenly a jailor who had heard us singing sprang into the cell.

10. "Sirs, what must I do to be saved?" he asked.

11. We told him in great joy.

12. "I can't do that," he said. "It's too risky."

13. As he left, he yelled over his shoulder, "Would you cut out the noise. It's three in the morning."

14. Still, I felt better for simply having praised Him. Praise clears the heart and dusts the mind of selfishness. It lifts the spirit and transforms the prison to an altar where we may behold the buoyant love of Christ. **15.** It is not jailors who make convicts. It is the self-pitying mind that makes a man a captive.

Praise frees us. The jail cannot contain the heart that turns itself to attend the excellency of Christ. **16.** "Gloria in excelsis!" deals with stone walls and iron bars in its own way.

17. When morning finally came, I was elated. I found a flint rock in the cell and scratched our own names above the etching of Paul and Silas: **18.** "Eusebius and Coriolanus—We sang at midnight and felt much better the next morning."

19. Was it foolish, Clement? **20.** It is always right to praise God, and maybe my inscription will help the next who occupy this cell to remember the principle, earthquake or not.

THE
FOURTH
LETTER
OF
EUSEBIUS
OF
PHILIPPI
TO HIS
BELOVED
FRIEND,
CLEMENT

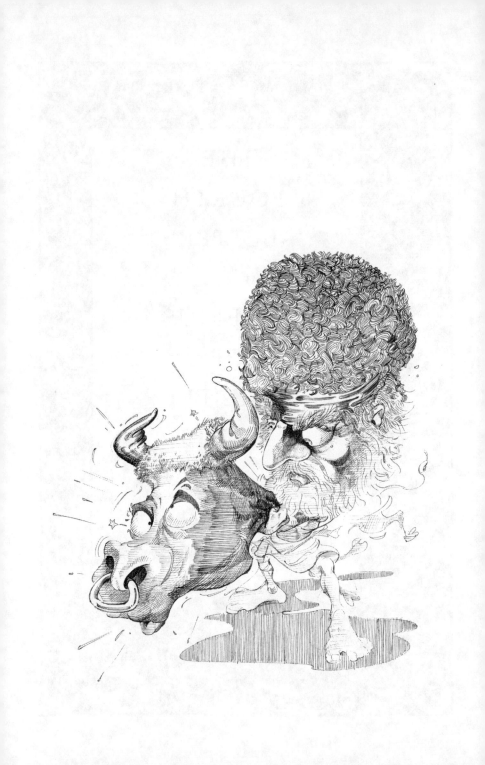

1

On the necessity of prayer

1. I am still in prison and disturbed by what goes on in Christianity. The God of the martyrs has gone sweet. **2.** There are some who are now teaching that God is a cosmic grandfather who gives to His children anything that they ask for if only they believe. **3.** Those who espouse it do not call it by the name I have chosen. They call it the Intercessory Prayer Movement. **4.** I cannot tell how many categories of prayer are being emphasized in the church now, but that is the popular one.

5. Prayer was not given to people to make them master over God. **6.** Yet, Clement, that is exactly what many in the congregation assume. If they pray, then God has to answer since they have asked Him in utter sincerity. **7.** It leaves God a dispensary attending his give-me communicants.

8. How in this egotistical school of thinking shall we ever have people who will seek

God for the pleasure of His company alone?
9. What an honor to find Him in a lonely moment and feast on the pleasure of our relation-
ship, which begs nothing because it has everything.

10. God is our friend. Who can keep a friend
who seeks only favors?   **11.** This leads to
what I would call the "Our-Father-who-art-
in-heaven-gimme-gimme-gimme syndrome."
12. It becomes a kind of celestial wishing before the throne of grace, ordaining Jehovah,
our fairy godfather.

13. I barely can stand this insult that leaves
God a baggage boy.   **14.** Our Lord did not ap-
proach His Father requesting a list of gifts.
15. He did not even seek bread after He had
fasted for weeks. He sought the Father because
He was God and there is no higher communion
than that.

16. Shall we not seek as He sought?   **17.**
Shall we not shut the door against earthly
noise and find that, once the noise is gone,
God will roar all about us?   **18.** It's the silent
communion of the closet that best declares His
reality.

19. The secret language of the heart never
heard by anyone else is the language of heaven.
20. But in the noise of life we can never hear
God.   **21.** Earth is so blatant that heaven does
not interrupt the noise with her music.

22. When we pray in public we speak so

much to others that God remains remote. It is the nearer audience to whom we pray. **23.** He only overhears our public prayers.

24. Once I heard a priest of Zeus read a prayer before a public sacrifice. He read it well, but not for Zeus. **25.** When you consider the object of the reading, you may be sure that if Zeus can hear he can also read. **26.** The Savior has reminded us that our heavenly Father knows our needs before we ask. As soon as the stylus scratches the paper, He knows what the prayer will say.

27. There are many admirable things about praying in public. But it is not the best kind of prayer.

28. It is closet praying which addresses God alone. **29.** Such prayer is itself a discipline, unattended by lesser ears or human compliment. **30.** May we meet Him in our loneliness to serve Him before the watching, listening world.

2

The prayer of Coriolanus

1. These are strange days of martyrdom and miracle. Our beloved Portia has gone to be with the Lord. She was facing the arena day by day, and while I do believe she would have

been victorious at the final hour, it never came.
2. Fearing the arena, she prayed to be delivered from the beasts and died of smallpox in her cell. So far the contagion has not spread, so we are rejoicing that Portia has been delivered.

3. While numbers have perished in the arena, there are victories from time to time. **4.** Urbanus wrestled the Taurus, Apollyon, and survived. Actually he broke the bull's neck, and the crowd was so impressed, they turned thumbs up and so he is back witnessing in the streets.

5. Urbanus is so popular that he has not been afraid to return to the jail. Best of all, he has taken over my work in the leper colony. He is so strong that he can carry Publius the Paralytic to church all by himself.

6. Phoebe is not afraid and visits the jail with news of the flock. She brings me the necessary parchment to continue my epistles. She really is a saint, and it is a miracle that she has not yet been arrested.

7. Circumstances are not so gracious for Brother James. He is down the lower corridor in a cell that has been called The Swamp. It abounds with lizards and such cell partners as few can endure. **8.** The guards have given him a small club to defend himself. And as we hear from time to time, he sings cheerfully in the cell and does not complain about his rather bountiful bedfellows.

9. There is a somber tone in the prison.

10. Last week the "event list" was handed through the bars. Coriolanus' name was one of the main events for the spectators at the matinee games. He was to be trampled to death by wildebeests. **11.** My poor adversary and current cell mate was clearly disturbed by the announcement. I wanted to suggest that we try to save his toga and sandals if he didn't mind going barefoot, but I took the course of compassion.

12. "We must pray, Brother Eusebius," he said.

13. "Amen, we must," I replied.

14. So we set our hearts to prayer. Daily he prayed for God to deliver him from the wildebeests. **15.** I suggested that he pray only for strength to face the deadly stampede, but he insisted on being delivered from the wild herd. So we prayed as he desired.

16. When the day came for his final witness to the faith, we were handed a note saying that he had been temporarily excused from martyrdom as the wildebeests had been smitten with hoof-and-mouth disease and were in no shape to trample Christians.

17. Coriolanus was ecstatic! "Glory! I have been delivered!" he cried.

18. Clement, he was snatched from the fire at the eleventh hour.

19. His near miss with martyrdom seems to have softened his arrogance. He owns, at least for the moment, a new humility. **20.** I know he must be growing in his piety for I asked him if he knew God's will for my life, and he had no idea.

21. He no longer speaks for God but is content to seek Him.

22. "When we are released, Brother Eusebius, I am going with you to take communion to the lepers."

23. "Excuse me," I said unable to believe my ears, "what did you say?"

24. "The lepers... Christ died for them too ... All are welcome at the table of the Lord."

25. "Coriolanus, you have not seen Lucia. Her hands and face are so eroded that the cup of our Lord's blood will come back as cankered and unclean as her bandages."

26. "Brother Eusebius! They are all God's children. What he has cleansed you must not call common or unclean. Lucia is our sister."

27. At that moment Phoebe entered the dungeon. The guard walked her to our cell, and then went back to his post.

28. "Coriolanus, you are still here," she said in amazement. "I don't understand. What of your sentence and the wildebeests?"

29. "They all have hoof-and-mouth disease," he replied.

30. "The saints be praised. I have brought

you communion," she said unwrapping a little tin cup of wine and half a loaf of bread. She extended the bread to me and Coriolanus took the cup.

31. "It is His body," she said to me. "It is His blood," she said to Coriolanus.

32. "It is His body!" I repeated, tearing off a piece of bread and putting it in my mouth.

33. "It is His blood!" said Coriolanus lifting the cup to his lips and beginning to drink.

34. As we took the blessed meal, Phoebe went on. "The lepers were kind. Lucia only drank a little from this cup. She left this much wine and bread to share with you and your cell mate, Coriolanus..."

35. Her sentence ended with the eruption of wine in the air all about us. Coriolanus spat, it seemed a thousand times, to get the wine from his mouth.

36. "You mean you took this very cup to the colony?" he asked.

37. "Yes, they are God's children."

38. "But they are diseased," he protested.

39. "Coriolanus, what God hath cleansed you must not call unclean."

40. There was a strange silence. I took the cup from Coriolanus and drank.

41. "It is His blood," I said.

42. It is strange how I believed Coriolanus. But it is even stranger that he believed himself free of the curse of fear and death. **43.** How often we make our greatest commitments only to be foiled by little adversaries! We will face the devil himself with courage and be bested by a crippled demon. We will face the wildebeests and quail before a communion cup.

44. Phoebe took the little bread and wine that was left and went to share the last portions with Publius the Paralytic.   **45.** In the remaining wine he will taste neither the leprosy of Lucia nor the hypocrisy of Coriolanus.   **46.** He will taste only the remembrance of a great deed long gone and feel good that consenting lips have been on that very cup before his own.

47. Thus is the church made one.

3

And of intercession

There has been victory throughout the church. Victor the Veterinarian was thrown to the lions only one week ago. Nothing like this has ever happened in the history of the martyrs.   **2.** Victor prayed for God to stop the lions' mouths.   **3.** When the great tawny beasts entered the arena, they advanced to Victor and circled him as though they would attack but then lay down, apparently uninterested.

4. Victor was happy about his deliverance.

But not the spectators!

5. When you pay three denarii for a seat, you expect to see someone eaten. The crowd booed and hissed, I can assure you. **6.** Finally they sent out thirty-two Asian lions who had been starved for a week. They ran up to Victor, sniffed all around him and then joined the others lying in the sun.

7. The Emperor was infuriated.

8. Twice more they released the big cats and twice more Victor's prayer tamed the huge beasts. **9.** Finally the crowd became so enraged they stormed the box office, determined to throw the ticket merchants to the lions.

10. It was a bad afternoon.

11. Sometimes you pay to see a game and there really isn't much going on. At least that is how the Romans have viewed the whole event.

12. But it has introduced a new question to the church. Consider the lone image of Victor the Veterinarian standing silently in the sea of big cats with his head bowed in prayer.

13. Victor has always had a lot of confidence in the power of prayer, and yet one cannot explain it all on this basis.

14. I remember Thecla of Thyatira who prayed to God to heal a little crippled boy from Bythinia. God did it, too. The little boy could walk and run ever after without the slightest limp. **15.** She was clearly a great woman of prayer, but her prayers, so often effective for others, could not finally avail for herself.

16. Thecla was arrested and sentenced to be thrown to the lions. Like Victor, she prayed to God to stop the lions' mouths.   **17.** The entire church joined her in the prayer. Nevertheless she was devoured before fifty thousand spectators.

18. She was truly a saint . . . as much as Victor, I think.

19. Why, then, would God honor one prayer but not another of the same kind? Who can say? **20.** Victor stands as proof to the entire church that God can answer any prayer for He has such power at His disposal for His people.   **21.** Thecla is proof that God does not choose to answer every prayer.

22. I have always heard it said that God may answer a prayer with either a "yea" or a "nay" or "one moment, please." Victor was back in the services this past week. Everyone there was glad to see him.

23. "What did you learn that day praying in an open field of big cats?" I asked him when he came to see me in prison.

24. "I learned," he said, "that God may be gracious to us and that he has all power to do everything that we ask."

25. As I turned away, he tugged at the sleeve of my tunic.

26. "One more thing," he said. "I learned

one more thing!"

"Yes?"

27. "It is always right to ask."

28. Clement, we may all come on hard times. We may all face terror of the beasts. But Victor is the proof that no matter how impossible the crisis may appear, "It is always right to ask."

4
Prayer in the Senatus

1. I am sure that you are aware that many martyrs in recent years have been arrested because a legionnaire discovered them praying in public. **2.** Now I have some disturbing news to report. I, too, once committed the blunder of spiritual indiscretion.

3. When I was pastor in Bythinia I was once arrested—for saying grace in a public park. I will never forget the sense of humiliation I felt. **4.** There I was praying for the fish and cheese and honey, and when I raised my head there was a centurion saying, "In the name of Caesar, come along with me."

5. "What is the charge?" I asked.

6. "Praying in a Roman municipal recreation area," he said curtly. It was years ago, but it was my first arrest and I have not forgotten the sting of it.

7. I was released in a couple of fortnights.
8. But it has led me to a lifelong examination of public praying.

9. Should Christians do it?

10. We are saturated with prayer as our way of life. There is a children's prayer that is now popular in Ephesus that goes:

11. God is great,

He made the trees.

Thank Him for the figs and cheese.

Bless *Mater*, and *Pater*,

and *Soror* and *Frater*.

12. We must be careful not to let the children pray where they might be caught. On the other hand, is it a coward's way out?

13. If the Empire has ruled against public prayer, should Christians continue to practice it or not? 14. Our Lord encouraged us to "render unto Caesar that which is Caesar's and unto God that which is God's." 15. But the Caesars don't believe that anything belongs to God. 16. One emperor defamed the doctrine by proclaiming his mount a proconsul, and ordering Romans to offer prayers to his horse.
17. The world is certainly confused when it is ordered to pray to a horse and arrested for praying to the true God.

18. But we must protect the children and at the same time encourage the church to be more in prayer than ever. 19. The times are vicious

and the consequences of our way of life must be considered.   **20.** I agree with our brother, Paul, who said, "I would that men everywhere pray"—whatever the consequences.

5

The church at praise and prayer

1. Clement, my entire parish is now convicts, or rather I should say, ex-convicts. The committee and all except the lepers and paralytics are finally in jail.   **2.** The good Urbanus brought Publius to the jail yesterday afternoon to see us. The old man was much more frail than I remembered.   **3.** His paralysis has been most unkind. But he is still a person of exceptional power in prayer.   **4.** When we came together, Publius repeated what I had already surmised to be true.

5. "The church is empty for the jail is filled with believers," he said, and then asked, "Where is our sister Phoebe?"

6. "Cell 32," I replied.

7. "And Dubious and Brother James?"

8. "Cell 70 and The Swamp respectively," I replied.

9. "Tonight at midnight I pray," he said.

10. "For an earthquake?" I asked.

11. Publius looked hurt at the cynicism in

my voice. "I'm sorry, Publius, but we tried that last month. We couldn't even crack the plaster."

12. "Tonight it will be different," he prophesied before he and Urbanus took their leave.

13. We all endeavored to keep faith with Publius, and so at midnight we began to pray. We linked hands from cell to cell and just repeated the words, "Jesus, the Son of God, is Savior of the church." **14.** As we repeated the phrases over and over, we felt a strange oneness.

15. Finally we shouted together, "JESUS THE SON OF GOD IS SAVIOR OF THE CHURCH!"

16. The floor began to move, then ripple. The ceiling began to fall and the bars twisted in the stone. Soon the whole place roared. **17.** The noise was horrendous; the splintering of stone and steel tore at our eardrums. The door of every cell swung open.

18. We all ran out into the corridors and then began to sing as we left through the stone arches at the end. The jailor was asleep. **19.** He may have been in a state of shock, but he appeared not to see us at all. We were all completely outside when I remembered the old inscription.

20. I tore myself from the group and reentered the prison. In the midst of the debris I found my cell and went quickly to the stones near the floor.   **21.** I picked up a flint rock and found the other etchings: "Paul and Silas" and then above that: "Eusebius and Coriolanus—we sang at midnight and felt much better the next morning."

22. I had to do it. Other Christians who might one day have the cell needed to know. I scratched my name and date just above the other two inscriptions and drew a crude arrow from my name to the names of Paul and Silas. **23.** I scratched a simple phrase beside the crude arrow:

"GOD DELIVERED US. KEEP THE FAITH."

24. I stepped over broken stones and rushed out into the starlight. Urbanus came out of the night carrying Publius who shouted through the darkness, "Did it work?"

25. "The jail is empty," I replied.

26. "The church is full," he cheered.

6

The arrest of Scrubjoy the Pure

1. Coriolanus seems to have returned to his former manner of life. His generosity toward me has seriously ebbed since we were cell mates. Still, the common ordeal of the church has generally freed us all from the dominion of any man.   **2.** Coriolanus suggested to me that while the pulpit at Konos no longer needed a pastor, there was a small church in Arabia. He now feels that God is leading me to pastor there.

3. The church has erupted with joy. **4.** Publius has just gone to be with the Lord, and we have buried him in a sunny field on the way to the leper colony. **5.** One must never be sentimental over the whereabouts of graves since to be absent from the body is to be in the presence of the Savior. **6.** Still, could he know it, he would love the field and the sun.

7. Urbanus has left the church and gone to Asia Minor to help with the work there. Phoebe and Lucia are working together among the lepers to extend the gospel among those who are not welcome in the city.

8. What can I say, Clement? The church services are marked by joy. **9.** It is so good to be preaching in my own church and to know that the peace of Christ which accompanied me to prison will now go before me.

10. Did I ever tell you what happened to Scrubjoy? He was far too open in his crusade against all sin. He built one of his famous "Purity fires" and was burning some "dirty scrolls." An old and scruffy tippler noticed the fire and wandered over to warm his hands.

11. "Scrubjoy, you old viper, how have you been?"

12. "Cassius! . . . I'm fine . . . I'm a Christian

now. I'm serving my sweet Jesus and taking my stand against all sin..."

13. "At once? Wouldn't it be better if you tackled one or two at a time?"

14. "No. God hates all sin and so do I." Scrubjoy threw a few more scrolls on the fire and watched them flame without smiling. "No, Cassius, my values have all changed.

15. "The axe is laid to the root of human folly. The time has come for all iniquity to be judged. The chaff is in the fire. **16.** All connivers, fools, adulterers and dancers will be thrown into the pit. Those who have made their tunics enticing and their evil habits an abomination will be judged."

17. Cassius looked at Scrubjoy through his bleary eyes. He hiccupped.

18. "You might as well know it, Cassius, your drunkenness is an abomination, too."

19. Cassius accepted his judgment in silence. Scrubjoy threw a few more scrolls into the flames and Cassius coughed as an unexpected puff of smoke came his way.

20. "Scrubby, what is Jesus like?"

21. "He is a great judge throwing sinners in the pit. He is the flame of the harvest that burns the evil chaff of this world. He despises low men and low morals. **22.** He sets on fire the course of nature till justice prevails and all men leave their evil wine and filthy minds in the devil's pit where they came from."

23. By this time Scrubjoy was preaching so loudly and his purifying flames had grown so high that a group of centurions noticed the light, heard the commotion and came to investigate.

24. "Wouldn't you know it, boys, another fanatic," said the centurion.

25. "Shall we arrest both of them?" asked a second soldier.

26. "No, just arrest the Christian. Leave the drunk alone. Drunks are pleasant people."

27. Well, Clement, Scrubjoy is the only member I have in jail at the moment. **28.** If he would just build smaller fires and fight a few sins at once, we might be able to keep him out of trouble.

29. Bear greetings to all in your parish who know me.

I commend you to Christ.

THE
FIFTH
LETTER
OF
EUSEBIUS
OF
PHILIPPI
TO HIS
BELOVED
FRIEND,
CLEMENT

1

The first of four souls—
Atticus

1. Atticus of Ephesus... no, Philippi... no, of Thessalonica... no, of Berea, has died. It makes little difference where he was from. **2.** He is in heaven now, or so we may hope. **3.** Let us be positive and pronounce him to be there.

4. He died at the Sunday Morning Games while most of us were at worship. He did not face the lions as a martyr. **5.** In fact, he had not gone to the games under persecution for his faith. He never openly declared himself a Christian, and that Sunday morning he cheered with the pagans the passing of his brothers.

6. For the last several years he had been overeating and overdrinking, and as you have already surmised, skipping worship for various amusements.

7. This particular Sunday he had gone to the games quite drunk and staggered awkwardly up the ramp during the main event where the Asian lions were loosed upon the African Christians. **8.** The Christians, as usual, were faring badly and Atticus turned to have a look near the top arena rail. **9.** He was bumped by a plebeian who was dashing for his seat and began to sway comically before he fell over the edge. **10.** The lions were on him in no time at all, and thus, against his good pleasure, he died in the faith.

11. So we may say our Brother has gone to meet the Lord. Let us assume that when he got there the Lord was not too upset about his untimely arrival. **12.** He was a member here in Philippi, but when I reported his passing to the rest of the fellowship, many of them asked me, "Atticus who?" **13.** It was then that I stammered the list of cities and empirewide addresses where the young man had from time to time been a member.

14. "Atticus who?" That is the question. I must admit that even I had to search my memory when the bereaved family requested his burial. **15.** "After all," they reasoned, "he began his Christian commitment in this church, so it is only natural that he finish up his Christian life at the same place."

16. During the next few days I attempted to reconstruct the life of Atticus from the time he disappeared from our church. **17.** I found that Atticus was visited many times because he was rarely in church on Sunday and avoided all mention of committing himself to anything. According to an old elder, the reason for his last departure was that he was asked to serve as an usher.

18. Atticus moved to Thessalonica where there was a large congregation. There it was easier to stay unnoticed. **19.** One of the Thessalonian deacons informed me that our late friend left in anger one Sunday morning when the pastor could not immediately recall his name.

20. From there Atticus went to Berea where he attended a service.   **21.** But his visit came on a Sunday when the sermon was on commitment and he never went back.

22. Some months later Atticus began attending the church in Apollonia, and it was there that he seemed most at home.   **23.** At least he remained long enough for nearly everyone to become acquainted with him.   **24.** In fact, he even organized a marathon team for the boys of the church. One of the charter members, Sister Penelope, accused him of poor spiritual leadership for the boys, and the phantasmic Atticus vanished again.

25. Two months later he re-emerged at Berea where he lived for years before he died as a Christian incognito. His nearly devoured remains will be delivered here tomorrow for burial. After all, is it not natural that one should end his earthly sojourn at the place it began?

26. I suppose his entry into heaven is a testament of grace. While I realize that nobody is ever worthy to enter those celestial halls, probably Atticus is less so than others.   **27.** Still, we must not be too hard on him. The lions, they say, had been starved to madness. The poor beasts were desperate.   **28.** The hapless Atticus was likely the first square meal they had eaten in a month.   **29.** While the committed martyrs may have tasted better, I suppose we must grudgingly admit that from the lions' point of view, what Atticus did for their hunger was a ministry of sorts.

2

*The second of four souls
–Sapphire of Cyprus*

1. Sapphire of Cyprus is getting ready to take her annual fair-weather leave. She has been polishing and oiling the wheels of the sporty new chariot she hopes to drive to her beach house on the Mediterranean.   **2.** She loves the summer and, while the weather is fair enough to permit witnessing along the Roman Road, she prefers to use the time for herself. **3.** She will arrive home in the fall with an excellent suntan and offer our Lord a lovelier complexion for her ministry among her paler sisters of this inland church.   **4.** Her tribe is becoming manifold. I grieve their absence in the fellowship. There are so many things that need doing for God, and so few available for the doing at certain seasons of the year.

5. But the Ides of May have come! Things go ill then that never go awry in the Ides of March during the winter solstice. **6.** I am tempted to be depressed by the coming of summer. **7.** Soon the trees will bloom and the birds throb with song. **8.** And what will the Christians do then? **9.** Many will join the coming exodus into hedonism. Their flight is on the heels of a winter which has lasted too long.

10. So they pitch their tents in the foothills of pleasure. By heaven, Clement, one must preach against this seasonal allegiance to faith. I'll not have it!

11. Shall we envy our brothers who soak in the sun and the sea? **12.** No. Let those who worship the sun burn in it! **13.** Woe to all whose leisure makes havoc of love! **14.** Woe to those for whom God is only a three-season deity! **15.** Woe to those who sun in glee, too stiff of knee to pray!

16. It is not that I would have men languish in the guilt of sacred summers. **17.** I cry to those who must withhold themselves from God and offer their bronzed bodies on the beaches of each lost Lord's Day. **18.** The voices of their Sunday infidelity rise from open-air indulgence crying their denial in the streets.

19. Woe upon our generation! **20.** Woe to the August of this heated infamy! **21.** Return, you rebels, from the sea lest God smite the shores on which you play!

22. Know this, O perverse generation, he who worships a nine-month God does not understand His unfailing foreverness. Autumn Gods are absent Gods. **23.** Clement, you may feel that I am harsh to these summer truants.

24. But I burn in the heat of this issue, and it is more than the Grecian humidity that makes me swelter. **25.** It is the seasonal apathy of the redeemed. **26.** Was our Lord's commitment to His Father's unflagging love only a seasonal affair? **27.** Sapphire of Cyprus and all the others of her ilk race to the beaches and leave behind them their ministry.

28. May hurricanes destroy summer! May the wheels break from their chariots! May their horses go lame! May vermin infect their figs and cheese! **29.** May they know only rain for the summer! But more than all else, may I learn to accept them and love them despite their sunny pilgrimages!

30. Enough! I am out of breath. **31.** Still, I am torn. Must Calvary's love be lost in sunsets and botany? **32.** One wonders what the Galileans were doing that April Friday when the cross was raised. Were they picnicing in Galilee on the shores of Tiberias?

33. That's the rub! We must learn to serve the whole year and worship the Christ of all seasons.

3

Bacchus and the problem of too much commitment

1. Occasionally I find a person who gives more to Christ than Christ wants. Some of these give more credit to our dear Lord than He would prefer.   **2.** I remember a sister who read the poems of Ovid and felt that she herself was a great Christian poet.   **3.** In her zeal she would read selection after selection of her work in the assembly and after each reading, she would demurely say, "The Holy Spirit gave me this poem; I take no credit for it of myself."   **4.** There was a widespread belief in the fellowship that the Holy Spirit didn't want the credit for it either.

5. It was not that she didn't mean well. Of course, she did. What is a Christian pastor to do to help those whose gifts are more limited than their zeal to use them?   **6.** They have a humility that is willing for God to have all the glory that their small talent may yield.   **7.** On the other hand, they have just enough arrogance to push their not-overly-sought-after talent on the undeserving.

8. My latest problem is Bacchus the Basso. He recently came to our assembly choir from the country chapel of Bythinia.   **9.** He boasted of being the best bass in the Bythinian brotherhood, having bested all other bassos in the back country.

10. How shall I liken his control and delivery? He is loud and deafening, like a clap of thunder in a stone tomb. He pumps too much of his melody through his nostrils.   **11.** His softness isn't soft, his vibrato doesn't vibrate and his precision is imprecise.

12. All these qualities are not as disturbing as his main affliction, his dedication.   **13.** He testified in the assembly that he just "had to sing for Jesus." By heaven, Clement, he'll have the Almighty with his fingers in his ears! And all the while he feels that he is doing heaven a service.

14. I have tried to dissuade him from using his gift. One elder suggested that he try ushering. Some are praying that the Lord heal him with laryngitis.   **15.** Others are coping by arriving after the music is over, just in time for the sermon.   **16.** If Bacchus continues, worship is done for in Philippi. The rodents left the building three solos ago, and soon the congregation will join the race of the rats.

17. You are far more skilled at diplomacy than I, dear Clement.   **18.** How does one tell a brother that his talent isn't, or that the gift he has laid on the altar of the Lord should have been laid to rest?

19. Willingness is an important quality in the life of a believer. It speaks against those who have gifts but are too stingy to make them usable.   **20.** Have you noticed that the greatest gifts often sit silent in a church while the poorest are exercised often and—as in the case at hand—in extreme.

21. I remember a certain alto sister who had been kicked by a taurus in the adenoids. She loved our dear Lord and sang violently to His glory. It may seem incredible, but she also was from the back country of Bythinia.   **22.** She would have perished in the first wave of persecution, but singing as she did at the hour of her death the lions would not go near her.   **23.** We were finally able to divert her talents into charity work among the earless lepers of Cenchrea where she is at the present time.

24. But of Bacchus I am not so optimistic. He is to sing again on the Lord's Day. Fortunately, I feel a flu coming on.

4 Petrus–the last of four souls

1. I want to get this letter to the courier on the southern sprint, so I must bring it to a close. But I would also like to ask your prayers for our church as it currently is.   **2.** My problems began some time ago, actually, but there have been certain deficiencies in our church programming since our latest stroke of ill-luck.

3. Two years ago a certain Petrus was thrown to the lions and the church at Philippi suffered terribly. It was not merely the grief that left our fellowship disconsolate.   **4.** The truth is that Petrus was busy, and his passing left a lot of holes in our church administration. **5.** Whatever do you do when your best committeemen are devoured?

6. Petrus not only taught a scripture class, but he was the keeper of the sacred purse, deacon widow tender, worship leader, and church greeter.   **7.** I know it sounds crass, but wouldn't it be nice if the lions devoured only the mediocre and nonactive members?   **8.** The beasts are chewing holes in our church structure.

9. I realize that the issue has not so much to do with the appetites of the lions as it does the current misunderstanding of discipleship.

It raises all sorts of questions. **10.** Did the late Petrus take upon himself much that other Christians might have done? Has the Arch-Enemy arranged it so that church workers who are unpalatable to God do not whet the appetites of lions either? **11.** Should only a few of the people do all the work? Can the problem be reversed? **12.** It is almost like the very arena in which poor Petrus perished. There were thousands of spectators looking down on a few people doing all the struggling. So it is from week to week in the churches.

13. And those who do all the work are often bitter because there is so little help. **14.** Take Petrus's widow. She died of nervous exhaustion only a couple of weeks ago. She too was an athletic Christian. **15.** She sang in the choir and played the lyricon for cherubs when they sang. She was janitress, deaconess, babysitter, and collected old togas for the poor. **16.** She ran atrium sales and baked squab for the visiting evangelists. It is hard to know whether it would be better to be eaten by lions or just collapse from the schedule.

17. It is said that when Petrus died he stared at the lion and said, *"Passio meus in Christi est."* (My suffering is in Christ.) It was all so lovely and noble. **18.** Petrus's widow on the other hand, just collapsed baking a pan of figgy bread for the women's group. Her last words were not directly translatable, although some thought it sounded rather like a grateful gasp.

19. Something must be done, Clement. There must be a better way to balance the work.   **20.** Some say there is a new wave of persecution coming, and the lions are hungry. **21.** I'm worried because so much of the work of the church is now being done by Julius. Were he to be devoured upon the Lupercal, we would be hamstrung at the church until the Ides of Janus when the new nominating committee meets for the first time.

22. Pray for us that more Christians here in Philippi will see their divine responsibility to become committed.   **23.** Pray that Julius will not be arrested for the Emperor's sport. We cannot stand the loss if we are to succeed in the current growth campaign.

24. The lions make it hard to keep our attendance where it should be.

25. Think of us at Lupercal.

THE
SIXTH
LETTER
OF
EUSEBIUS
OF
PHILIPPI
TO HIS
BELOVED
FRIEND,
CLEMENT

1

The world is coming to an end along with patience

1. Who can deny that the world is coming to an end, soon and abruptly? 2. There are many indicators, "signs of the times," as they are all prone to say in the streets. 3. This is truly a time of transition, the worst time—I think—that the world shall ever see. 4. Never has there been a time so short of time as our own. These are the last wretched days of the putrid, planet earth.

5. Am I overdoing this, Clement? Keep in mind that there is the hint of universal winter in the air. The night is upon us. 6. The Gauls have marched into Germania and are holding the natives at swordpoint. 7. Here at the very height of the Iron Age the Britons are raising the price of ore again. We shall soon not be able to afford rims for our chariot wheels. 8. Complicating the peace is the Nubian protest. The orb is restless.

9. Is this the last dark hour? Some are saying

the world will not long endure and that our very Caesar is the Anti-Christ. **10.** They say that Gaul is the Great Gog of Ezekiel, and that the conflict over iron will lead us at last to the battle of Armageddon. **11.** Some are saying that the century will never see its close before doomsday dawns.

12. What do believers do when they are confronted with perilous times? All ages are ages of transition, and soon give way to the next.

13. We Christians are frustrated by these times. We have forgotten our birthright. We are citizens of the world to come. **14.** Should the planet itself come to an end, we could get by without it.

15. The other day I passed a little man carrying a sign that read: "The World Is Coming to an End!" I thought to pass on down the street when I heard a sickening thud on the cobblestones behind me. **16.** A runaway chariot had skidded into the sign bearer and crushed him. **17.** They picked up his frail, old bones and threw him into a cart and then tossed the sign on top of him.

18. It was somehow symbolic. Do not most messages end with their messengers? **19.** We should check our own pulse and respiration every time we diagnose the terminal diseases of our planet. Nor should we stand when we are sick with a high fever to talk about the death of the age.

20. The world itself may be old, but the prospect for the life of the believer is joyous and new. Forgive me if I am not as morose as others seem these days. **21.** God seems well enough. **22.** I shall post this small epistle, believing it will safely reach you before the end of all flesh shall come.

2

The urgent ministry of Quintus Quick

1. My own concern about these desperate days has been sparked by the furor around these itinerant preachers of Christian doom. **2.** They are not entirely gloomy, of course. They feel all believers will escape without a scratch in the glorious rapture of the church before the battle of Armageddon begins. **3.** I should like thinking that Philippi will not shortly go up in smoke, but if it does, it's nice to know that the millennium dare not begin until I am snuggled in at the throne.

4. Quintus Quick is in town and says that the day of the Lord is upon us. **5.** "Get ready! ... Get ready!" he thunders out over the heads of the hearers. **6.** "The great beast is about to make his mark on every forehead in Northern Greece ... Woe to those who receive the mark!"

7. How are we to adjust to his desperate

urgency?

8. The day of the Lord is surely nigh. The signs of the times are all about us. **9.** Our blessed King is coming again soon. MARANATHA! We are eager to see Him. Each morning I find myself looking east and asking the question, "Why not today?" **10.** But I always feel a certain uneasiness in this immediacy. **11.** The preaching of Quintus Quick has caused no little stir among the believers here. **12.** He has written a devastating scroll called *The Late Great Date of Human Fate!* He has drawn a great number of historical parallels between the book of Daniel and the current time. **13.** He feels that the Roman Empire is the great ten-horned beast of the Apocalypse and that the angel has already begun to pour her golden vial on the sun and that the age is shortly to end.

14. Last night an ardent brother asked if the Lord could come back before all the Jews returned to Jerusalem. **15.** While Brother Quick felt that this was not possible, he did feel that the great whore, drunk with the blood of nations, would probably prevent the two witnesses from sharing their midtribulation testimony. **16.** "This," he said, "could cause a kind of satanic infection in the third toe of the great beast, and some of the ten horns would then decline in size as the scarlet rider begins her charge across the world with her pillaging and death."

17. Several were alarmed at Brother Quick's message that the Abomination of Desolation was already becoming obvious. **18.** He said that the livid horseman of Revelation was none other than the current grain shortage in Thyatira. **19.** This famine would be used by the new satanic trinity to draw men and women to commit adultery with the golden idol of time, symbolized by the great statue of Nebuchadnezzar in the book of Daniel.

20. His lecture tonight is entitled, "Who Is Gog?" **21.** He has promised to reveal the mysterious identity of old Six-Sixty-Six. **22.** I guess it will be nice to get a little inside information on the Anti-Christ, but somehow I am insecure about Quintus Quick. **23.** His crusade in Philippi and other cities has made him a lot of denarii. He can now dress in the best togas. When the rapture comes he will surely float upward in the best of threads, leaving the planet in class.

24. But he does seem consistent. The sticker on the bumper of his chariot reads clearly, "In Case of Rapture, This Chariot May Become a Runaway." **25.** I suppose if the Second Coming occurs tonight, Quintus will be whooshed away with the rest of us. He will probably be a little sad, however, to have to end his dynamic series on the subject.

26. It is always hard to wait for the Second

Coming, Clement. I'll write more later; right now I'll go and plant an apple tree. If Quintus Quick is wrong, I may someday enjoy its fruit.

3

On the problem of relics

1. It has not been more than a few decades since our Lord walked the planet and there are now hundreds of souls making trips to the Holy Land in search of relics of one kind or another. **2.** Last year Zelpha of Iconium found a board that was supposed to be a part of the cradle where Christ slept as a baby. Being somewhat of a devotionalist, Zelpha kisses the wood each morning; then holds it up toward Nazareth and prays in the name of the Infant King. **3.** She is certain God hears her prayers and even if He doesn't, the board sure brings her good luck.

4. Last year between Easter and Whitsun several relic peddlers came through selling everything from a martyr's tooth to a feather from Gabriel's left wing. **5.** I ask you, how can they tell it was his left wing? What shall we say to these things? **6.** When does the worship of holy things at last supplant the worship of a Holy God?

7. But here is the grand problem. Lavinia

came on the Lupercal displaying the holy cloth. She says this sacred cloth is the very towel used by our Lord to dry His hands on the way to the cross. **8.** If you look, you can still see the imprint of His blessed hands on the towel, she says.

9. When she came to church last Sunday, she was followed by a crowd of pilgrims, singing and swaying in adoration for the "Holy Hand Towel." **10.** The towel had once been in the possession of Barbara of Berea, who was barren and whose barrenness was the bane of her dear Brutus, who always wanted children. **11.** Well, Barbara laid the towel across her barren body, and behold, she conceived in her womb. **12.** She and Brutus have been blessed with a baby boy whom they have named "Bartus of the Holy Hand Towel." **13.** Not only that, but Barbara washed the holy cloth and hung it on a dead tree limb to dry, and when she went to bring it in again, lo, the dead tree had brought forth leaves and flowers.

14. She gave it to Lavinia who once was plagued with warts, but since the holy cloth has been in her keeping, her skin has become clean and pure without a blemish.

15. Should Lavinia come to Coos, she will let you see it for three mites or touch it for a shekel. This is the way she has chosen to finance her holy ministry. **16.** This slight charge has allowed her to trade in her old chariot for a new one, and she plans to build a prayer tower down by Rhodes financed by the proceeds from the pilgrims.

17. Soon Lavinia wants to take the towel on a healing tour of lower Greece.

18. Clement, do you think the towel could have any real powers? It does seem strange that since Lavinia has owned it, she has rarely spoken of our dear Lord.   19. Wherever she goes, they fall down before the cloth, but few are coming to faith.   20. Christians who used to praise God now only say, "Wow!" "Wow" is a new word I hadn't heard before. It's meaning is unsure, but I think it expresses more wonder than praise.

21. Let us beware of such shallow adoration that the world may turn from relics to reality.

4

A new discovery and its effect on the fellowship

1. We are in such a quandary here in the church to know exactly how to deal with those who from time to time receive the gift.   2. I must confess, dear Clement, that I myself have prayed to receive the gift, ardently and long. But so far it has never come.

3. The problem is that those who have received it wonder at my lack of excellence.   4. It

is hard, indeed, for a pastor to live with such a reputation when others have received it. **5.** The latest in the congregation to reach this plateau of spiritual excellence is Dolores of Delphos.

6. Dolores has received *the gift*. She has been praising God often and loud, sometimes standing in the middle of my sermon and shouting syllables of joy. **7.** She smiles constantly, weeps much and in general has many wishing her gift was still wrapped.

8. Dolores went to a women's gleam group depressed and came back smiling. She has been smiling ever since. **9.** Even when she had a fever, she smiled, praised God and raised her hands till all her bracelets fell to her elbows.

10. Her experience has been a little difficult to understand. It is her praise phrases that seem to nettle the less emotional brothers in the fellowship. **11.** She "blesses God" regularly. **12.** For instance, she was introduced to a new member of the church, and when it would have been entirely appropriate to say, "Hello," she "blessed God!" **13.** When she was told of the death of Hyrum of Pisidia, she once again "blessed God."

14. But "blessing God" is not her only idiosyncrasy. **15.** She abounds in "praise phrases." "When you're distressed, seek to be blessed!" Or several have heard her remark, "Precious Jesus, heal our diseases." "Lift up holy hands, Brother!" is another of her phrases.

16. Now it seems that her affectation is shortly to become an infection. She has been trying to organize spiritual gleam groups in the church. **17.** For a while some were glowing. Sister Priscilla thought she had the gift, but after three days of smiling she had to sit down and rest. **18.** Aphia of Antioch also smiled for a day and a half, but an early elbow injury kept her from holding her hands up for very long; she is dropping out of her gleam group and joining a Christian discussion club. **19.** Patience is threadbare. We cannot force ourselves into the irreverent position of telling Dolores that her gift is grating on our group. Never has the quiet love of God been so blatantly obvious in the church.

20. What are we to do? Since Dolores got interested in her new joy, she has scarcely had time to minister to the sick and the lost. All her energy is expended on blessing God and starting gleam groups. **21.** Her happiness seems all right for her, but it is clearly driving the church up the *arbor insectus.*

22. And who gets all the credit for her eternal smile? The Holy Spirit. **23.** Can this be the same Holy Spirit sent to comfort us in times of grief?

24. There's the rub. Grieving is as much a part of life as gleaming. How can we give the giddy, ever giggling Dolores a balanced view?

25. Jesus was serious at times. Four times the scrolls say that He actually wept. We showed Dolores the very passage that said, "Jesus wept," but she only smiled and blessed God and handed us an invitation to the next gleam group. **26.** We are at an impasse.

27. Some other epistle I might close by saying, "Bless God," but things being what they are, I think I'll just say, "Have a pleasant day."

5

The lepers

1. I am in need. Three of our wealthiest members had their homes and goods confiscated by the authorities, and thus, the church income has declined. **2.** Before my conversion in Asia Minor I used to make sandals and leather boots for the legionnaires. Well, I have gone back into the work again. **3.** My hands have suffered terribly. The leather is often hot and the huge needles have cut savagely into my palms. **4.** I am sure that they will toughen and that before long I will be able to work faster.

5. I had enough scraps left from my first four pair of sandals to make a left thong for Lucia the Leper. **6.** How I suffer in knowing that the dear woman, even if she could afford to, must always buy her sandals one at a time! I cannot tell you the joy on her face when I took her the new shoe. **7.** She has been a leper for twenty years, and the disease has not been kind to her. She has a wealthy daughter in Philippi who could take her all she needs to ease her stay in the colony of the damned. But she hasn't heard from her daughter in three years.

8. "Tell me, Brother Eusebius, would you cross the Neapolis Road and see if you might inadvertently catch a glimpse of my daughter in the garden?" she asked when she had finished lacing up the thong on her left sandal. **9.** "If I could know my daughter was still alive and in good health, I could go to my grave in peace. She just never could tear herself away from the comforts of Olympian society to face the risk in being a Christian.

10. "The last time I saw her," the old woman went on, "was the year I lost my right foot. She had just been to the games during the high persecution and was thrilled that so many of our brethren were being destroyed. **11.** How much it hurt me, Brother Eusebius, to hear her so critical of the martyrs. She told me then that the sooner the whole Grecian Peninsula was cleared of our heresy, the sooner the gods would bless the land with rain and new crops..."

12. She hesitated and turned away. At

length she spoke. "Come!"

13. She hobbled off on her right crutch and new left sandal. "I have been selfish," she said over her shoulder as I followed.   **14.** When we reached the back of the hut she pointed to a bronze box hidden by the foliage. She sat down suddenly and drew out the box with her gnarled hand.

15. "Will God forgive our selfishness?" she asked.

16. "He forgives all," I answered.

17. "I have kept this far too long. It is all I have owned of any value. I have kept it for no reason except it was mine and it is new. I will not be guilty of storing up trifles. Do you know Delia who lives in the mud thatch near the cemetery?"

18. "Yes. I have heard that she is considering becoming a Christian."

19. "Then you have not heard!" she exclaimed, overjoyed about the news she was to impart. Her face was alive with spiritual radiance. I no longer saw the contagion that scarred her face.

20. "Delia *is* a Christian now!"

21. I smiled as a kind of weak mirror to the radiant joy of Lucia.

22. "Here, you open it!" She handed me the bronze cask. Her malformed hands throbbed with excitement.

23. I hesitated a moment to reflect on this

episode of joy and the mystery of the box.

24. "Well, go on," she insisted.

25. I opened the box. In it lay a single sandal.

26. "I put it here when my condition became so bad that I could no longer walk. Then I lost my right foot. This box since that time has been a shrine of self-pity. **27.** When my daughter ceased to care about me, I came only to dote on my desolation. But when you gave me this sandal just now, all that changed. **28.** Leprosy is but an earthly category. Delia says that in all the anthems of the crystal city they have never heard the word "unclean."

29. "It is true," I said.

30. She ran her hand across her face, "Then the only scars in the new eternity are those which mark the hands of Christ."

31. We sat for a moment; then I put the sandal back in the case and started to leave.

32. "No, No!" she protested. "Take it to Delia. It is a small token for our hope. Do you know where her hut is?"

33. "I can find it!" I said.

34. I made my way through the brush feeling the new joy my old occupation was providing. Back in the sandal business after all these years! How can we ever know that Christ himself may hide in so simple a thing as a sandal.

35. I was lost in thought. Still swinging the simple gift, I saw Delia's hut. Lucia's strange token held a meaning I did not understand.

36. I caught sight of Delia squatting outside. When she saw me, she rose up and leaned against a leafless tree.

37. Then I knew. Delia was standing on her right foot. It was bare.   **38.** Her left was gone.

39. The love of one leper may sometimes keep thorns from the foot of another. And in a world where two amputees are required to make a single set of footprints, eternity is a welcome word.

6 *On Nicholas the Liberal*

1. You will pardon the smudges on the parchment, but I have been getting some oil together for the big burning.

2. Nicholas the Liberal is to be ignited at the seventh watch today.   **3.** Nicholas has been teaching doctrines unfriendly to the faith, so I'm afraid he must be burned.

4. Burnings are not what they use to be since oil is in such short supply.

5. Clement, I do not like these burnings. They are no witness to the love of Christ. **6.** Nicholas has denied the key doctrines, and the faith can scarcely exist if his kind of heresy is tolerated.   **7.** Yet I feel uneasy in these events.   **8.** I cannot believe that God is altogether pleased.

9. I remember last year when we burned Brutus Dubitus.   **10.** His wife and children were crying so you could hardly hear the choir singing "Love Divine." It took much of the dignity out of the occasion.   **11.** Brutus preached in the Chapel of Errors before he was arrested by two of the Fiery Faithful. **12.** They said his views of Scripture were unsound.   **13.** As they lit the oil, Brutus began to sing the praise of Christ.   **14.** Now I have a feeling that he may have been burned by mistake.

15. I believe every word of Scripture, and I hate to hear it maligned, but I am nervous. **16.** A certain narrow saint heard me preach only a fortnight ago and told the Fiery Faithful that I was strong on the Incarnation but never once referred to the Transcendent Holiness.   **17.** Clement, could we be burning tomorrow's heroes before the facts are in? **18.** Now there are rumors about me all over Asia.   **19.** Should you be asked to bring the oil to my burning, I would have you understand I do not doubt the Word.   **20.** We have to stop burning each other or we shall leave our finest witnesses in the ashes.   **21.** It does no good to sing of love while we grind our teeth. **22.** Nor is it easy to whip the error-ridden into hell while we try to preach the way to heaven.

23. It is a mad world where Romans burn Christians who, in the pursuit of good doctrine, burn each other.

24. Hark! I hear a knock at the door. Good doctrine be forever! It is the Fiery Faithful crying for my blood, "Where truth is spurned, men must be burned." **25.** I must bury this letter under the floor before I answer. The stake may await me.

26. Should I never see you again, Clement, we shall meet in greater light.

7 Four to three

1. Clement, wonder of wonders, I have been acquitted at my heresy trial. The Fiery Faithful were somewhat divided in their assessment of my theology. I was acquitted by a vote of four to three. **2.** After the trial we all sang "We Are One in the Bonds of Jesus' Love." It's a beautiful hymn, but all the time I was singing, I just kept thinking, "Four to three!"

3. After Nicholas was found guilty, they sang the same hymn before the burning. Again the vote was four to three.

4. I believe, however, that the Fiery Faithful will soon cease their witch hunting, for the persecution is gaining in intensity. One of them was thrown to the lions only yesterday, in fact, to seven lions at once. **5.** Three of them showed no interest in devouring him, but four tore him to pieces.

6. May all the lions vote in my favor if my time should come. Clement, pray for me as I do for you, in these perilous times.

THE
UNFINISHED
EPISTLE,
THE
LAST
KNOWN
LETTER
OF
EUSEBIUS
TO
CLEMENT

1. Clement, the time of my departure is at hand.   **2.** Even now through the iron grating of my arena cell I hear the hungry snarling of the big cats.   **3.** I am slated to fight it out with the African lions. Fight it out? What real chance is there—the lions always win.

4. Clement, how much over all these years have I enjoyed our friendship! Although we were forced to communicate across so many miles of desert, mountains and open sea, how surprising it has been to find all of the things that we have had in common! Our tastes, our petty grievances, our fondness for integrity, our admiration of the ideal.   **5.** How shall I ever thank you for your letters? And now, dear *amicus*, the lions shall stop our correspondence.

6. For me our letters have been a useful outlet. Knowing that you read and sometimes shared my troubled experiences has made it easy for me to be open and honest.   **7.** Brother, though I have sought to be, I am not that brave in the pulpit.

8. I am not a brave man—not even a man who finds it easy to talk of the supernatural, faraway, spiritual realm you find so near and natural. **9.** I am just a doomed commoner who, given a fondness for the here and now, nonetheless believes all he can. I always feel the crunch of being trapped between what was and what I would rather have been.

10. The truth is, the times were too desperate for the luxury of orderly and logical thinking. But I struggled for it. **11.** I faced my own weaknesses and found that I tried to love God with a faith that was often too practical to be deep and too timorous to be courageous. **12.** I am frightened to the depths.

13. I have not experienced the martyr's syndrome. I have gone through shock, anger and acceptance. **14.** I was shocked when I first was notified. "Why me?" I protested to the Almighty. **15.** A voice spoke out of the darkness: "Eusebius, it's just your lucky day! Think of the joy it will be to beat all of the nonmartyrs to the fullness of heaven!"

16. Then I went directly into anger. "Look, God," I said, "you've got the wrong man! I'm not that dedicated!"

17. Clement, they say that your name's sake, Clement of Alexandria, at his arrest looked steadfastly into heaven and said, "I go now to Rome to become the bread of God, made from meal, ground between the teeth of lions." How sweet and how beautiful! **18.** How pleased the Almighty must have been with this lovely, poetic anticipation of a noble death.

19. I am never going to be one of those little sugary, prayer-filled martyrs who sings hymns as he is torn to pieces. **20.** I will embarrass God running and crying before the lions. It's going to be a bad show. I love God but am afraid of animals. **21.** I remember when Antipas was devoured, he cried, *"Sola Christus vita mea est!"* How spiritual compared to my "Let me out of here!"

22. Clement, my anger has turned to bitterness. It just isn't fair! I have dealt with Coriolanus and the deacons. I have carried bread to the lepers. I have preached in prison. **23.** And what do I get for all this? Nothing. The lions are the winners. All of my dedication to the ministry ends as a meager serving of fodder.

24. I could have been a success if I had worked for Jupiter. His priests pronounce the invocation at the very games where we are devoured. **25.** These pagan priests laugh in the streets that their invocations are really a kind of table grace for the beasts. **26.** In truth I can not think of the lions and pray, "Lord, bless my body to their body."

27. Oh, Clement, this is my last letter. It is all over! **28.** Your final vision of me will not be as you have always thought of me. No, no, no! You will see your dear friend running pell mell from the animals and crying in terror. Where's the dignity in Christian death?

29. I am praying moment by moment for the Second Coming. It would be the best way out for both God and myself.   **30.** Then the lions could go back to eating whatever they ate before Christ came and hapless martyrs believed.   **31.** I have been very tense lately, Clement, with a lot of chest pains. It could be my heart. This morning I experienced a massive pain that stopped my breath and seemed for a moment to paralyze my vision.   **32.** It could be serious . . .

To Clement of Coos:
I found this letter addressed to you laying by the body of Eusebius who was discovered dead in his cell. Had he lived one more day, he might have been a gallant witness to your God. He spoke constantly of Jesus, and rarely in his last week of life did the jailors pass his cell without hearing him at prayer. Even in the face of martyrdom his disposition to his keepers was congenial and his faith was intriguing to us all. He believed with such force that we who kept his cell were almost convinced to join him in faith. If he was right in his visions, he has now joined a hope we Romans have tried in vain to challenge with lions. If he was wrong, I yet envy the joy his faith provided.

Sincerely,
Lucilius
Arena Warden

AFTERWORD

Who Is Helmut Niedegger?

In February 1970 I was invited to a three-day colloquium of archaeologists held in Baltimore. My interest in this particular conference was immense because several papers were to be read on the gnostic gospel of St. Thaddeus which had been found the previous year in a wine cellar in Beirut. The manuscript was clearly a forgery, but it was a third-century document composed near the end of Diocletian's reign of terror.

When I arrived on Monday, I was disappointed to discover that the first paper on the gnostic gospel would not be read till Tuesday. I might have stayed away from the opening symposium altogether except for the title of the Monday night seminar: "Egyptology, Assyriology and Coosiology in Perspective." It was the word *Coosiology* which arrested my attention. I had never heard of the discipline. I ran my finger down the list of lecturers and was surprised to find not just one paper but three on the subject, and all were to be read by Helmut Niedegger of Leipzig Library. Dr. Niedegger was to read his first paper at the close of the Monday night session.

Fatigued though I was, I went to the opening of the symposium. The first two papers addressed Egyptology and Assyriology respectively. They were plodding. Besides, I was familiar with these disciplines. But Coosiology was such a new field that most of those in attendance were locked in rapport with the small German scholar as he delivered his paper. I was fascinated to discover that Coos, which Dr. Niedegger always pronounced Ko-os in two syllables, while the rest of us continued to rhyme it with "moose," was in more modern times called Stanchio, an island with many pigeons. It was once a major island in the Aegean. The apostle Paul, legend has it, had weighed anchor there on one of his missionary journeys.

Dr. Niedegger explained that he had come to believe that there existed somewhere on the island near the monastery of St. Thaddeus a second-century manuscript written by Eusebius of Philippi during a horrible wave of empirewide persecutions. He himself had searched for this manuscript for more than thirty years but had never been able to find it. He believed that it was hidden somewhere in the vaulted archives of that monastery. He mentioned that the monks of St. Thaddeus not only took an oath of silence like Trappists but actually consented to having their tongues torn out. This assured them that they would never be tempted to break their holy vows. Since this was a small Eastern Orthodox monastery, they wrote only in Greek and never spoke at all. Dr. Niedegger believed that the lost manuscript might have been easier to find if the communication barrier had not been so great.

After the delivery of his outstanding paper, "Coosiology and The Lost Documents of Philippi," I, like thirty or forty others, had an overwhelming desire to touch the eminent scholar. For reasons that I now believe may have been uniquely inspired, I had the good fortune to be staying at the very same hotel as Dr. Niedegger. In a city the size of Baltimore this can hardly have been a mere coincidence. Thus our fellowship tightened into esteem during our three days together. Dr. Niedegger filled me with a growing appetite to visit Coos and to obtain, if I could, any information at all about the lost Philippian document. While I knew that the manuscript would not be directly related to the New Testament era, I began to believe that it was a key to understanding the general era of the early church fathers.

I took Dr. Niedegger to the airport in Baltimore. He had to deliver The Eastern Research Lectures at the Smithsonian Foundation before he returned to Germany. "Goodbye, Calvin!" he yelled back in a broken German accent as he walked down the jetway, "If you need me, you can write me at the library in Leipzig!" he said, melting into the queue of passengers.

"Auf Wiedersehen, Helmut!" I yelled after him. Standing a moment, looking wistfully away, I turned on my heel and walked out of the airport. Dr. Niedegger had awakened an idea within me that would not sleep.

I arrived in Coos (please forgive me for not using the modern name of the island) six weeks later. The island was much as Dr. Niedegger had explained it. I had flown in on a sea plane from the harbor at

Rhodes and, after taxiing on the dockside, hired a cab for my trip to the base of Mt. Arphaxad. Once I reached the base of the mountain, I began the steep ascent to the monastery of St. Thaddeus that could only be reached by foot.

When I was finally inside the compound, two monks showed a look of panic and rushed upon me as though I was standing on forbidden holy ground. They seized me and began shoving me toward the stone gate by which I had entered. "Unhand me, Brothers!" I shouted to the silent and brutish holy men. They continued shoving me until I cried out, "I am a personal friend of Helmut Niedegger!" At the name of Niedegger they fell backward as if they had seen an angel. They bowed before me and rose again. With kinder faces they led me back into the compound.

There were now only twenty-four monks at the monastery, all committed in silence to their years of ministry. A novice showed me the library, kitchen and wine cellar. Another showed me to a small, crudely furnished room. It was apparently the guest room, for as I stepped inside, they made mute gestures of welcome as though they wanted me to stay there.

Only two items hung from the walls—an ivory crucifix and a photograph of none other than Helmut Niedegger of Leipzig Library. As they bowed to leave the room, they genuflected not before the crucifix but before the portrait of Helmut.

I will not detail how my next two months there were spent. Among the silent brothers of St. Thaddeus I became the close friend of the Abbot Androcles. After some time he encouraged me through the unique sign language that had developed at

Mt. Arphaxad to search for the missing manuscript
which Dr. Niedegger had mentioned at the colloquium in Baltimore. Even if it were important to
tell of this search, it would not be expedient. It is
sufficient to say that every niche and cranny of the
dusty monastery was searched. Everywhere I
looked I well imagined that the Librarian of Leipzig
had already been there. I was disappointed and was
soon convinced that my search could not avail. I
made preparations to return to my parish in the
Midwest since I knew my congregation would soon
be wondering what had become of their pastor.

On the day I was to leave the most fortuitous
event of my life occurred. The Abbot Androcles
had ordered the wine vat enlarged in the third-
century enclosure directly beneath the stone larder
that had been built in the twelfth century. During
the removal of the stones, a large leather bag was
discovered. In the bag was a scroll which the Abbot
Androcles gave to me.

While the scroll was attached only to one spindle,
it was obviously substantial. The uncial Greek
characters ran together in a manner typical of
second-century manuscripts. I was delirious!
Across the opening vertical column of faded black
letters ran the words, *To Clement of Coos from Eusebius of Philippi.*

I assured the Abbot that I would give proper credit to the brothers of St. Thaddeus for the discovery
of the piece if only he would let me take it to Leipzig
and share the joy of its discovery with Helmut
Niedegger. At the mention of the Coosiologist the
Abbot released the scroll to me.

I changed my travel plans and flew directly to
Leipzig, having wired the council of the church I

pastor, telling them that they must wait two more weeks for my return. I knew that they would understand when they learned of my discovery and of the importance of my consultation with Dr. Niedegger.

Once in Leipzig I took a taxi to the university and went directly to the library. After I reached the small, neat German campus, I entered the library and asked the receptionist for directions to the study of Herr Professor Doktor Helmut Niedegger.

"Niedegger?" she asked.

"Helmut Niedegger?" I repeated my question. "He is here, of course," I added, impatient with the Fraülein.

"I'm sorry, Sir, we have no Niedegger on this faculty.... There's a Mr. Neidenstein who cleans up the place...."

"I'm sorry, Miss. I'm speaking of Helmut Niedegger, the eminent Coosiologist," I said in my broken German.

"The Coosiologist?" she repeated the word as though we were playing some sort of game and then winked at what she obviously considered to be our little secret. "Why don't you try the Coosiology lab, my good fellow."

I was furious. But in an entire afternoon of searching, I found no mention of Helmut Niedegger in any part of the School of Antiquities or any other faculty. No one had ever heard of him. Could I have been crazy? Did he not deliver the key papers at a great American symposium on archaeology? Did not twenty-four monks in the Aegean worship his picture? A man of this stature simply does not drop out of the intellectual circles that sired his reputation. Yet no one in the university knew anything about Niedegger nor, indeed, of the discipline of

Coosiology.

Disheartened I returned to America where I set to work translating what I came to call *The Philippian Fragment*. It was clearly a partial scroll and I needed the rest. I knew that somewhere sometime there had existed another spindle with more of the precious document wound around it. When I submitted the manuscript to the Department of Antiquities at the Smithsonian Institute, they declared it a forgery and surmised it had been scripted by a calligraphy student in the art department at Baltimore Metrotech. When I talked to the curator on the phone, he assured me that it was a bogus document. I felt ashamed and then cautiously asked him if he was familiar either with Dr. Helmut Niedegger or Coosiology.

"Coosi-what?" he asked.

"Never mind!" I said, hanging up the receiver.

A week later I received a list of criticisms of the manuscript. Most scholars had rejected it on the basis that the existence of a coliseum in Philippi was highly dubious and that the monastery of St. Thaddeus mentioned in 1 Clement 1:13 could not have existed in the second century since monasteries were produced in a much later day. Besides, the critics said, no monks in Christian history were ever known to tear their tongues out to enforce silence.

I returned to Coos for the proof I needed to establish both the reputation of *The Philippian Fragment* and my mentor, Helmut Niedegger. I arrived at Mt. Arphaxad in June 1974. The monks were glad to see me. They wanted to know how Helmut Niedegger was faring in Leipzig. I couldn't bear to offend them, so I assured them that he was just as alive and well as a man of such renown and age could expect to be. They were pleased.

The Abbot Androcles, who seemed much older than before, motioned me to the back room and gave me a towel in which was wrapped the other spindle and the rest of *The Philippian Fragment*. I could hardly contain my joy. Then he took me to the chapel of St. Thaddeus and we had a special mass of thanksgiving for the discovery of the other half of the uncial scroll. I photographed the Abbot Androcles and his twenty-three brothers to use as proof of the existence in Christian history of tongueless monks. I also photographed the picture of Helmut Niedegger that hung across from the crucifix in my room. I intended to staple this to the old program that I had still retained of the Baltimore colloquium so that Coosiology and the Coosiologist could be restored to their rightful prominence in the world of archaeology.

Who can know the reason for all that befalls us? My last night on Coos I decided to stay in a beachfront guest house. I had packed early in the afternoon, taken the other half of the manuscript and left. That very night Mt. Arphaxad was destroyed by an earthquake. The monks were all buried in the rubble. The portrait of Dr. Niedegger was destroyed. In the aftermath of looting and confusion, my hotel room was burglarized and my camera and all the exposed film were lost.

When I returned home, I translated the remainder of *The Philippian Fragment*. Now that it is published, I suppose it will become a laughingstock in archaeology. During the past five years I have sought to locate any mention of Helmut Niedegger in the world of scholarship, all to no avail. I deeply regret the lack of esteem that exists for my work and especially the life work of my missing mentor.

Now that I have finally found a publisher who believes in my work (the editor smiled when he told me that), I only plead that you, dear reader, will see the intrinsic merit of this magnificent document. If after your study of this volume you still believe it to be bogus scholarship, I ask you to answer one question for me: Who is Helmut Niedegger?

Calvin Miller
Omaha, Nebraska

CALVIN MILLER

Calvin Miller is a graduate of
Oklahoma Baptist University and
holds the Ph.D. from Midwestern
Baptist Seminary. He is currently
a pastor in Omaha, Nebraska,
and is the author of *Once upon a Tree,
Poems of Protest and Faith, Sixteen
Days on a Church Calendar,
Burning Bushes and Moon Walks, A
Thirst for Meaning, That Elusive
Thing Called Joy, Transcendental
Hesitation, A View from the Fields.* His
most well-known work is *The Singer
Trilogy (The Singer, The Song, The
Finale),* a poetic retelling of the
story of the New Testament.

The cover and interior illustrations
are by Joe DeVelasco, a Chicago
artist whose innovative work also
accompanies *The Singer Trilogy.*